# This Woman's Work

# This Woman's Work

## The Writing and Activism of

# Bebe Moore Campbell

Osizwe Raena Jamila Harwell

University Press of Mississippi / Jackson

*Margaret Walker Alexander Series*
*in African American Studies*

www.upress.state.ms.us

The University Press of Mississippi is a member
of the Association of American University Presses.

First printing 2016

∞

Library of Congress Cataloging-in-Publication Data

Names: Harwell, Osizwe Raena, author.
Title: This woman's work: The writing and activism of Bebe Moore Campbell /
Osizwe Raena Jamila Harwell.
Description: Jackson : University Press of Mississippi, 2016. | Series:
Margaret Walker Alexander series in African American studies | Includes
bibliographical references and index.
Identifiers: LCCN 2015044828 (print) | LCCN 2016001783 (ebook) | ISBN
9781496807588 (hardback) | ISBN 9781496807595 (epub single) | ISBN
9781496807601 (epub institutional) | ISBN 9781496807618 (pdf single) |
ISBN 9781496807625 (pdf institutional)
Subjects: LCSH: Campbell, Bebe Moore, 1950–2006—Political and social views.
| African American authors—Biography. | Authors, American—20th
century—Biography. | African American women political
activists—Biography. | Social change in literature. | Race relations in
literature. | Mental illness in literature. | BISAC: SOCIAL SCIENCE /
Women's Studies. | SOCIAL SCIENCE / Ethnic Studies / African American
Studies.
Classification: LCC PS3553.A4395 Z53 2016 (print) | LCC PS3553.A4395 (ebook)
| DDC 813/.54—dc23
LC record available at http://lccn.loc.gov/2015044828

British Library Cataloging-in-Publication Data available

This book is dedicated to the health,
wholeness, and wellness of us all.
Let us continue our work of healing, forgiving,
and sharing our gifts with the world.

# Contents

# Acknowledgments

I am grateful to have so many communities and sources of rich support. This project simply would not have been possible without the kindness, expertise, and sacrifice of so many amazing people. First and foremost I want to acknowledge my editor, Craig Gill, and the wonderful team at the University Press of Mississippi. I could not have asked for a more encouraging, patient, and reassuring editor. Thank you for your great confidence in this work and guidance each step of the way.

Nathaniel Norment Jr., Valerie Smith, Nikol G. Alexander-Floyd, Daniel Omotosho Black, Layli Maparyan, Abu Abarry, Muhammed Ahmed, Sonja Peterson-Lewis, Patricia Melzer, Bettye Collier-Thomas, Pamela Barnett, James Davis—collectively you have guided me on the path of excellent scholarship, excellent research, and excellent character. Thank you for your powerful example.

Throughout my writing process many friends offered accountability, writing dates, proofreading, printing services, and a critical eye to make this book the best it could be. Kami Anderson, Mari Laela Mitchell, Ayanna Jones, Takiyah Nur Amin, Miriam Petty-Adams, Mei Campanella, Khaia Smith, Cedric Smith, Kanika Bell-Thomas, Jonathan Gayles, Sarita Davis, and Makungu Akinyela—you made rough places smoother, and I love you for loving me so much! I want to say a special thank you to Vanessa Jackson, an amazing power coach and adviser, for ensuring that I stayed the course in positive, healthy ways.

I am grateful for my lineage of love and power: my fathers James Seku Harwell and Clarence Milan; my brothers Zaire L. Harwell, Kendrick Scales, and Tiq Milan; my grandmothers Julia Bolden and Florine Harwell; and my "othermothers" Janice Rounds and Rosemarie Norment. To the Harwell, Bolden, Milan, and Scales families, you are my foundation, a place to which I can always return when I am in need. To the Spiritual Living Center of Atlanta and the Nation of Nzinga and Ndugu, thank you for growing me—continually and lovingly—to share my gifts, to heal, and to love freely. I am fortunate for family, and I do not take for granted those who continually shower me with kindness, affirmation, meals when I am writing, a compassionate ear, a good laugh, or a warm hug. Thank you to so many loved ones, too many to list, but whose names are etched in my heart.

I am extremely grateful to all the friends, family, classmates, and colleagues of Bebe Moore Campbell for sharing your memories and to the Archive Service Center at the University of Pittsburgh. Ellis Gordon, Doris Moore, Linda Wharton Boyd—I thank you especially for welcoming me inside your homes and your hearts. To Bebe Moore Campbell Gordon—your vision, your power, and your voice have truly touched the world, and I am *more* than grateful for your life and your legacy.

Finally, my most heartfelt appreciation to my mother, Dolores Bolden-Milan, for your endless praise, financial support, cards sent in the mail, gentle criticism, and a million hours spent pouring over draft after draft with me as I revised this manuscript. In every encounter you are love personified. "Thank you" is woefully insufficient, and I fall short in every attempt to express my gratitude in words, but I know that you know!

# Introduction

On November 27, 2006, journalist, activist, and award-winning novelist Elizabeth "Bebe" Moore Campbell died at the age of fifty-six after a short battle with brain cancer. Although the author was widely known and acclaimed for her first novel, *Your Blues Ain't Like Mine* (1992), there has been no substantive study of her life or of her literary and activist work.[1] This book examines Campbell's activism and writing, highlighting two periods of her life—as a student at the University of Pittsburgh during the 1960s black student movement, and later as a mental health advocate near the end of her life in 2006. In this work, I also engage Campbell's first and final novels, *Your Blues Ain't Like Mine* and *72 Hour Hold* (2005), and the direct relationship between these novels and her activist work. This critical biography is not a "tell-all" of Campbell's personal life; it is an exploration of her writing, public service, and activism. Nonetheless, I do examine the ways her personal life, family struggles, and relationships inform and interact with her literary, journalistic, and activist work. Ultimately, I explore the personal and leadership characteristics that distinguish Campbell as a significant writer-activist who produced effective outcomes throughout her life work. I argue that these characteristics are sometimes overlooked, but are central to the discourse on black women's contemporary activism. As a writer, Campbell utilized recurring signature themes within her novels to theorize and connect popular audiences with African American historical memory and current sociopolitical issues. I purport that, through her literature, we learn more about Campbell, her politics, her personal life, and her public work for social change. Essentially, I offer a close study of Campbell's work within organizations and a deep inquiry into her writing as an activist tool. Thus I provide the reader with a greater understanding of what Campbell does as an activist, and what her writing does to advance the social change she envisions.

There are numerous black women writers who exemplify excellence, influence, and literary innovation. In the 1960s and 1970s (in step with the Black Arts and black liberation movements), black women writers like Nikki Giovanni, Toni Morrison, Sonia Sanchez, Audre Lorde, Toni Cade Bambara, Alice Walker, and Gayl Jones forged a foundation for female writers to come and left a rich legacy of literary excellence for the next generation. Out of this explosion of black women's literature emerged Bebe Moore Campbell, alongside "sister writers" like Pearl Cleage, Octavia Butler, Terry McMillan, Diane Whetstone McKinney, Tina McElroy Ansa, Lorene Cary, and several others who stand on the shoulders of their black literary foremothers. Thus, with the continuous proliferation of notable black women writers since the 1960s, one might ask, "Why study Bebe Moore Campbell?" As a writer and activist, Campbell has used each of her works as a powerful vehicle through which subject matter is enlivened and expanded, thus immersing her readers in relevant historical and sociopolitical phenomena.

This examination of Bebe Moore Campbell's life and work posits that she is a figure worthy of critical attention because she is an important writer whose fiction addresses race, culture, and identity, as well as the past and present sociopolitical experiences of African Americans; she writes for popular audiences yet also engages sociopolitical commentary and African American historical memory in narrative fashion; and her early and more recent activism and related writings exemplify effective and substantive work toward social change in the United States. Overall, her critical lens is both appealing and accessible to broad audiences among the general public. In academic settings, her novels are a useful complement to nonfiction instructional texts in the college classroom.[2] For scholars, Campbell's intellectual, creative, and political work adds to the legacy of and the growing discourse on black women's activism of the recent past (particularly within social movements of the mid-twentieth century) and on black women's activism in the contemporary period. In addition to articulating sociopolitical discourse, Campbell's novels often include elements of African American historical memory, effectively integrating the contemporary popular fiction with nonfictional themes and subject matter.

This book is informed by the burgeoning study of black women's historical and contemporary activism and addresses gaps in women's studies and black studies. Works such as Kimberly Springer's edited volume, *Still Lifting, Still Climbing: African American Women's Contemporary Activism* (1999), began to detail the sociopolitical activity, personalized narratives, and intellectual production of black women. Springer's later work, *Living for the Revolution: Black Feminist Organizations, 1968–1980* (2006), departs from individual activists to focus on political activism in black women's group formations. Belinda Robnett's study, *How Long, How Long: African American Women in the Struggle for Civil Rights* (1997), is useful for considering black women as "bridge leaders" who strengthen the constituency, infrastructure, and longevity of social movements, rather than subordinating their contributions and their primacy in the work for political and social change.

Methodologically, I stand with Margo V. Perkins's *Autobiography as Activism: Three Black Women of the Sixties* (2000) as she examines the writing of black women activists as a way to understand their sociopolitical ideas and involvements. Whereas Perkins analyzes the autobiographical writing of Assata Shakur, Elaine Brown, and Angela Davis, I examine the fictional writing (which has its own autobiographical leanings) of Bebe Moore Campbell.

In the turn toward the examination of single subject in the study of women's literary, artistic, and activist work, Maria DiBattista (*Imagining Virginia Woolf: An Experiment in Critical Biography*, 2008) and Farah Jasmine Griffin (*If You Can't Be Free, Be a Mystery: In Search of Billie Holiday*, 2002) offer compelling biographies of important female cultural figures. Both authors extend beyond narrative and chronological biography to deliver analytic, thematic, and sociopolitical accounts of their respective subjects. This critical biography moves in a similar direction with a single-subject consideration of Bebe Moore Campbell's life, activism, and writing.

On occasion, some scholars of literary studies seek to maintain a canonical boundary that discounts the value of contemporary literature, popular fiction, and black writers. Works like *The American Dream and the Popular Novel* by Elizabeth Long (1985) have challenged this exclusionary trend. Long argues for the social significance and literary value of popular fiction and rejects the notion that only certain works are worthy of serious intellectual consideration (that is, those penned by predominant white and male authors of earlier decades and centuries). In my study of Bebe Moore Campbell, a notable best-selling novelist, I continue the challenge to such "literary gatekeeping," which leaves many black women writers in the margins, by exploring the intellectual and practical importance of black vernacular fiction. To be clear, it is necessary to recover Campbell's fiction from the dismissal of black writers who are oriented toward popular audiences. As other works in the past three decades have begun to seriously engage the value of popular literature and figures, such as the study of romance novels by white female authors (see Tania Modleski's *Loving with a Vengeance: Mass-Produced Fantasies for Women* [2008] and Janice Radway's *Reading the Romance: Women, Patriarchy, and Popular Literature* [1991]), this shift is especially urgent within African American women's literature. As I clarify throughout this work, Campbell's novels, in addition to their literary value, function as dialectical text with value for scholarly and mainstream audiences alike.

Campbell was widely acclaimed and celebrated as a popular writer, yet in the development of this project I encountered varied opinions from academic colleagues on the scholarly value and literary quality of her work. When I discussed the research I was proposing, some were generally familiar with Campbell, others were disinterested, and a few were as excited and enthused as I was. Many people were unaware of the expanse of her body of writing and wide readership. They even dismissed her work as "bourgeois and middle-class chick lit" (that is, lacking urban "grit" or authenticity) or "beach chair" literature (that is, something you would read at the beach or just for fun), thus lacking in literary value, seriousness, or social relevance. After reading some of my work on Campbell, a white female liberal arts professor who was familiar with African American literature said to me: "I don't really like her myself—and I have used her work in my class. But you know . . . she is no [Toni] Morrison."[3] This comment exemplifies the very sort of intellectual snobbery that I would like to explode with this project. Besides the fact that this professor—and most detractors (black or white)—hadn't read all of Campbell's novels, her personal opinion was subjective and unsubstantiated by any sort of viable critique or argument. The comment was also ironic since Bebe Moore Campbell, in her own right, garners high esteem among her peers and progenitors in the field of contemporary African American literature.[4] Moreover, because Morrison is of an earlier generation than Campbell, such a comparison is out of context. Toni Morrison is someone Campbell names as one of her favorite writers and role models, rather than a peer or contemporary. Ultimately, such elitist notions within the academy position authors against one another and exclude popular writers whose work is more accessible to mainstream audiences. It is unfortunate that this "high art" approach establishes such narrow confines of which works are considered classic, which works can be classified as "literature," and which are worthy of serious scholarly consideration.

Nonetheless, the news of Campbell's death in 2006 was followed by reverberating celebration of her literary and social impact.[5] The undisputed acclaim that accompanied her passing suggests that this work and other scholarly projects on this important writer-activist are necessary and relevant. My examination of Bebe Moore Campbell is, in part, an attempt to trouble the waters and highlight the type of written work that is at once complex, easy to read, critical, accessible, and popular. In addition, this book seeks to engage the writer's sociopolitical strivings and personal activism, thus rearranging the boundaries that exclude popular writers from serious scholarly attention. Campbell's published writing reflects a direct association to her lived experience with activism and service to black communities. I examine the reflexive relationship between her literature and her social activism, thus establishing new terms for canonical inclusion of black women novelists and writers of African American popular fiction. As I examine Campbell's work, I argue that black women's vernacular writing is unarguably literary, intellectual, and distinctive.

To discuss Campbell's activism and writing, I utilize the concept of *framing*,[6] a central concept in the area of social movement theory. Framing considers the way that leaders help people understand an issue or cause in such a way that draws greater participation and sustains this participation over time. I contend that Campbell's activism, writing, and intellectual development reflect the process of *frame alignment*. That is, through writing and other activist practices, she effectively amplifies, extends, and transforms sociopolitical concerns specific to African American communities, engaging a broad range of readers and constituents. As a student activist in her college years and a mental health activist in her adult life, Campbell's dynamic leadership style was central to bringing attention to important causes, drawing constituents to get involved, and maintaining involvement over time. I elucidate Campbell's formal and informal leadership roles within two social movement organizations. In conjunction with her deliberate use of writing as an activist tool, I conclude that in both activist periods Campbell's effective use of resources, personal charisma, and mobilizing strategies aided in grassroots/local and institutional change.

Black women scholars, including Belinda Robnett (*How Long, How Long*) and, more recently, Nikol Alexander-Floyd (*Gender, Race, and Nationalism in Contemporary Black Politics*), utilize framing and social movement theory in similar ways to expand black feminist scholarship on social movements and black politics. Their application and discussion of frame alignment processes provide a precedent for this project, which explicates the nature and value of Bebe Moore Campbell's writing and activism. Alexander-Floyd uses the framing paradigm broadly to discuss frame alignment outside of the context of social movements.[7] She identifies frame shifting to define problems and policies within contemporary black politics. Frame shifting departs from the focus on a social movement organization and focuses on an intellectual, ideological, or political movement across processes: shifting, amplification, extension, and transformation. Frame shifting is ultimately a change in one's conceptual location. Robnett extricates her central premise from frame alignment theory and social movement theory to challenge the mislabeling of black women's activism in the civil rights movement as supporters rather than leaders. She advances the concept of the *bridge leader* who is essential to the success of a social movement and often facilitates the frame alignment process. Bridge leadership, as described by Robnett, draws from the first process of frame theory, known as frame bridging. Robnett zeroes in on the many ways bridge leaders draw and maintain their constituency over time and minimize the issues that lead to a decline in activist participation. Throughout this work I reference frame theory and bridge leadership to discuss the nature and process of Campbell's literary and activist work.[8]

In addition to the use of social movement theory as a tool of analysis, it is also important that I clarify my own sociopolitical and theoretical standpoint. As I conducted research for this project, womanist and feminist labels were debated and applied to Bebe Moore Campbell and her work by colleagues and study participants. I have had to consider these projections thoughtfully and to grapple with the importance and the politics of naming. I have concluded that I am most interested in what an activist (or project) *does* rather than labeling activists as part of a single ideological camp. I find labels and identifications are relevant, and I realize that labels and categories change, that values change, and so on. Thus I translate these labels to verbs and adjectives that describe Campbell and explain her actions, rather than nouns that place her in a feminist or womanist identity group. Accordingly, there is a plethora of relevant antisexist theories that can be applied to Campbell's writing and activism.

In Part I, the holistic, spiritual, and communal nature of her activism is well suited for applying a *womanist analysis*.[9] In Part II, I apply a *black feminist analysis*[10] to discuss the racialized and gendered themes that Campbell incorporates in her novels. I don't find these two frameworks to be in conflict with one another—although misunderstandings arise when popular definitions replace their theoretical meanings and nuances. Overall, I engage the antisexist nature of Campbell's work; I clarify how gender, race, and, occasionally, sexuality find their way into her sociopolitical commentary. I discard the debate of whether Campbell "was a feminist" or not and "why she is more of a womanist" instead. More urgent than theses labels are the precise connotations of antisexist theories they describe as we realize the importance of her labor. To be clear, the standpoint I take is an antisexist lens that departs from ideological divisions, thus allowing different elements of Campbell's writing and activism to be understood with the most useful theoretical tools available.

Unlike a traditional biography, my analysis allows readers to get to know Bebe Moore Campbell by exploring her life's work. While Part I is loosely chronological, I narrow in on two significant periods of her adult life, and in Part II I offer an in-depth examination of the writing and activism that she cultivated as a novelist. Methodologically, I used oral history interviews, primary source document analysis, and textual analysis of the two novels to examine and reconstruct Campbell's involvement and her influence as a student activist at the University of Pittsburgh and as a mental health advocate and spokesperson for the National Alliance on Mental Illness (NAMI). I draw on Campbell's midlife memoir *Sweet Summer: Growing Up with and without My Dad* (1989) for its early biographical profile, and extend the biographical narrative with personal interviews that I conducted with her family, friends, and colleagues. I consider public interviews and speeches by the author to give primacy to her personal voice and articulation of her work and her intentions. Finally, while I was unable to interview Campbell's daughter, Maia Campbell, I reference the actress's personal interview with self-help guru Iyanla Vanzant. On Vanzant's Oprah Winfrey Network television show *Fix My Life*,[11] Maia addresses the impact of her mother's death and the toll Maia's mental illness has taken on her and her family. The episode also features Maia's stepfather, Ellis Gordon, and her own daughter, Elisha (Bebe Moore Campbell's husband and granddaughter). Maia's mental health experience is especially relevant here because her diagnosis and care are the primary catalyst and inspiration for Campbell's dedication to mental health advocacy. Campbell's novel *72 Hour Hold* is loosely based on her experience as a mother struggling to find resources and support for her daughter with mental illness.

This volume is organized in two parts. In Part I, I offer a biographical treatment of Campbell's activism in two periods of her life. In Part II, I explore Campbell's writing, with a literary analysis of her first and final novels. The two parts work together to examine her lived activism along with the intellectual biography drawn from her career as a novelist. Campbell's committed activism existed in concert with her contributions as a writer. Examining the nature of these two areas of work offers an integrated understanding of Campbell as prominent writer-activist.

In chapter 1 I begin by examining Campbell's early activist experiences at the University of Pittsburgh during her formative years as a college student. Specifically, I zero in on the influence her early activism and political consciousness had on her later activism, writing, and advocacy. I describe Campbell's leadership within the Black Action Society (BAS) from 1967 to 1971 and her negotiation of the black nationalist ideologies espoused during the 1960s. In chapter 2 I shift to the activism of a middle-aged Campbell from 1999 to 2006, which centers on a very personal family matter. In the narrative of her ascent from concerned parent to national spokesperson and local organizer for NAMI, we see Campbell utilizing the similar strategies of relationship building and inspiring others to forward a social cause that began in the BAS at the University of Pittsburgh. However, she also uses her fame and celebrated writing career to "amplify" the issues of mental health awareness in black communities.

In chapter 3 Campbell's first novel, *Your Blues Ain't Like Mine*, is correlated to her emerging political consciousness as a college student (specific to race and gender) and the concern for racial violence during the black liberation period. The examination of recurrent themes in *Your Blues* reveals a direct relationship to Campbell's activism at the University of Pittsburgh. Similarly, chapter 4 engages Campbell's last novel before her death, *72 Hour Hold*, which has a chilling resemblance to her own life and offers new insights for understanding and living with a loved one who has mental illness. *72 Hour Hold* is examined closely for its sociopolitical commentary and emphasis on mental health disparities, coping with mental illness, and advocacy in black communities. I connect the devices and sociopolitical imperatives of Campbell's last novel to her involvement in NAMI, her role as a national spokesperson, and the local activism that sparked the birth of the NAMI Urban Los Angeles (NULA) chapter serving black and Latino communities.

In the epilogue, I close the volume by considering the lessons and resonant features of black women's activism in the contemporary period as exemplified by Campbell and her cohorts. I suggest that there are new implications to be drawn from their examples that call forth the redefinition of activism in the context of support networks and the practice of regular self-care. Through her writing and activism, Bebe Moore Campbell comes forward as a significant bridge leader concerned with various sociopolitical problems.

Together, the analysis of her activist work and her novels provides an intellectual biography that narrows in on Campbell's literary work and her direct involvement in social change movements. It also establishes a precedent for scholarly examination of African American women writers marketed to popular audiences and adds to the study of African American women's contemporary activism, health activism, and black student activism. Overall, the following pages promise to engage the reader in the intriguing story of this woman's work.

# Part One

Campus Activism and
Community Mental Health Awareness

# The University of Pittsburgh and the Black Action Society: Campbell's Early Years as a Student Activist

*My mother was a social worker and I grew up with a lot of social workers for friends. And the era, the backdrop for my life was the civil-rights movement. So that comes quite naturally to me.*
—Bebe Moore Campbell, interview by *Time*, August 6, 2005

Born Elizabeth Moore on February 18, 1950, in Philadelphia, Pennsylvania, Bebe Moore Campbell grew up in North Philadelphia on the heels of the civil rights movement. She attended public city schools at the height of *Brown v. Board of Education* and school desegregation.[1] When Campbell was seven years old her mother, Doris Moore, enrolled her in the newly integrated Logan Elementary School. Campbell recollects being one of a handful of black children in attendance and the high expectations from her mother and grandmother. In her memoir of her childhood, *Sweet Summer: Growing Up with and without My Dad*, she recalls that "Nana and Mommy like most upwardly mobile colored women, believed that to have the same education as a white child was the first step up the rocky road to success."[2] She recalls her grandmother's stern and loving words on the first day of school: "Act like you've got some home training. You've got as much brains as anybody up here. Do you know that? All right now. Make Nana proud of you."[3] Campbell also tells of spending each summer in rural North Carolina with her father and paternal grandmother. Through these annual trips she experiences the black rural culture and African

American folkways associated with the South. She juxtaposes these visits with her North Philadelphia upbringing, where she was reared by her mother and her maternal grandmother. At an early age, Campbell observes the contrast and diversity of African American experiences with racism, poverty, work life, and family values. She experiences the distinctions between the black South and her urban northern inner-city black life in the 1950s and 1960s. Campbell remembers her childhood fondly, emphasizing the stern nature and work ethic of her father and North Carolina grandmother, alongside the local Philadelphia neighborhood full of parental figures who nurtured her along the way. Growing up in the wake of the civil rights movement had a profound impact on Campbell and would eventually inform her career as a writer. In an interview, Campbell once recalled the impact of Emmett Till's murder as child and feeling unable to "let it go":

> I was five when he died. He was a topic, and still is, in my community. He was a reference point. I'd hear my dad talking about him, or he would come up in conversations with my uncles, or somebody would mention him, and I just felt as though I knew this boy. He could have been my big cousin. He was not an historical figure. He was not like Harriet Tubman or Sojourner Truth or Frederick Douglass. He was my age just about. So, I always thought of him—the outrageous injustice of the way he died—as sort of symbolic of the oppression of African Americans in this country. He was always in my mind. I felt as if I knew him, and I like the historical as a jumping off point.[4]

Till's murder was so significant that it would become the inspiration for Campbell's first novel, *Your Blues Ain't Like Mine*.

Both of Bebe Moore Campbell's parents came from humble beginnings. As first-generation college graduates they instilled their only child with high self-esteem, an early social awareness, and a value for education. Doris Moore received a scholarship to the University of Pennsylvania, pursued a master's degree, and became a social worker. George Moore informed his parents that he had no interest in being a physical laborer and wanted to pursue college. Moore attended North Carolina A&T University and became a local farm agent and entrepreneur.[5] Campbell's parents ensured that she was on the path to college and personal success with high expectations, and by enrolling her in best public schools in Philadelphia. Bebe attended Philadelphia High School for Girls (also known as Girls High). This public preparatory school is the alma mater of other greats such as Jesse Redmon Fauset, Elaine Brown, and women who would become mayors, White House fellows, merit scholars, Ivy Leaguers, and all-around high achievers.[6] After graduating from Girls High, Moore attended the University of Pittsburgh, where she studied elementary education. Campbell's stable upbringing by socially conscious parents who placed an emphasis on education and community would make Campbell a vocal and active presence on her college campus during the 1960s black student movement.

During the summer quarter of 1968, a small group of students gathered on campus at the University of Pittsburgh to address and respond to the growing concerns of the black student population.[7] Earlier that year, on April 4, 1968, the entire nation was rocked by the assassination of civil rights leader Martin Luther King Jr. As was the case throughout the country, students at the University of Pittsburgh initiated the work of correcting racial inequities and tensions on campus. Undoubtedly, these students were cognizant of the rising black student movement at colleges and universities throughout the United States, and in like fashion, on May 19, 1968, the Black Action Society (BAS) was formed at the University of Pittsburgh.[8] Campbell's participation in the BAS occurred at a heightened point within the black student movement when, across the nation, student activists were organizing, making demands, and protesting inequities and social injustices on college and university campuses. This period of the black student movement was concerned with three primary issues: the relationship between the academic institution and the local black community; an increase in black student enrollment and the hiring of black faculty and administration; and a curriculum overhaul that included and accurately depicted African American history and culture. The last issue included the associated demand for black studies departments and programs.[9] Campbell had enrolled at

Pitt in the fall of 1967 and was among these founding students who had remained on campus for the 1968 summer quarter when the majority of students had gone home until the next fall.[10] The season that followed the informal dialogues among the summer students would be marked by a flurry of organizing, protests, collectivism, and political consciousness raising. This small group would ultimately transform the university and the countless students who were in attendance during this turbulent time. Campbell's involvement in black student activism prefigures her future work with mental health activism in black communities.

The nature of critical or intellectual biography is to reveal more about a subject's thinking—his or her theoretical and creative work. It also considers the relationship between a person's work and his or her personal life. Upon close examination, many of the themes and approaches to Campbell's literary work parallel her activist involvement at the University of Pittsburgh. Consequently, there is a correlation between the sociopolitical discourse of the period and the emergent themes in her first novel, *Your Blues Ain't Like Mine*. As will become clear throughout my analysis of Bebe Moore Campbell as an important cultural worker, the salient ideologies of the student activist period dynamically shaped her later work. Her contributions as novelist resonate with the strivings and the multiple movements of 1960s black liberation. Beyond her writing, Campbell's interest in and campaign for mental health awareness in black communities demonstrate that she was political both with her pen and in practice. Thus her political participation and active role in on-campus programming foreshadow the ongoing sociopolitical activism and commentary evidenced throughout her life. In order to glean a more grounded understanding of Campbell's involvement in the BAS at Pitt, let us first consider the national climate of the 1960s black student movement.

Campbell attended college in the late 1960s, which was a particularly robust period in US history. Given the national context of sociopolitical change, the on-campus climate of growing racial and cultural consciousness, and her membership in the BAS, what can be said of Campbell's experience as a student at the University of Pittsburgh in the 1960s? Entering college at age seventeen, Campbell brought her early experiences of growing up in North Philadelphia at the height of the desegregation era, and was one of the first to enter integrated schools in the city. Campbell was well prepared for college, having graduated from a leading public school and being reared by a mother, father, and grandmothers who deliberately strengthened her confidence and leadership skills. As a working mother, Doris Moore closely guided and supported Bebe's personal and academic development up until she left home to attend the University of Pittsburgh.[11] Accordingly, she arrived at the university as a focused, disciplined, and conscientious student. Still, the freedom and maturation that accompanied her college years would take her in new directions and areas of growth altogether.

For African Americans, this decade yielded multiple movements for social, political, and economic change on the heels of the civil rights movement. After many successes and failures, the civil rights movement would give way to a more assertive and self-affirming season of overlapping struggles for equality and justice. Thus the era of "black liberation" included the civil rights movement, the Black Power movement, the Black Arts movement, the black studies movement, and the black student movement. The civil rights movement of the 1950s was primarily concerned with discrimination, equal rights and access, and desegregation. Alternatively, the Black Power movement rejected nonviolence, confronted police brutality, and articulated a pro–black stance that rejected integrationist aspirations in place of community building and institution building. The Black Arts movement complemented Black Power discourse by producing creative works and by theorizing the role and function of black aesthetic production to black liberation. Campbell's coming of age during these major movements, and the strong sense of pride garnered by her family, clearly precipitated her involvement in student activism on her college campus. The later phases of 1960s black student activism (also referred to as the black campus movement) followed in the steps of student activists in civil rights groups like the Student Nonviolent Coordinating Committee (SNCC) and the Congress of

Racial Equality (CORE), but focused on campus-centered activism (campus activism often extended into the local community as well). Black student activists primarily protested, boycotted, and made demands for African American faculty, relevant curriculum content, responsibility to local communities, and the formation of black studies departments at American colleges and universities. Subsequently, these movements merged as a juncture for the institutionalization of African American studies as an academic discipline; thus the black studies movement emerged as an effort toward bringing black liberation to the American educational system. While none of these movements can really be extricated from the other, the black studies movement is directly linked to black student activism on college campuses. A black studies curriculum would become one of the key demands of Campbell and her colleagues at the University of Pittsburgh.

The synchronicity of the historical moment would bring Campbell and her classmates into the historical narrative as the black collegians would follow in the steps of their young black liberation movement predecessors and the campus movements that began to spring up around the country. In general, the broader scope of black student activism begins with the civil rights and Black Power movements of the late 1950s and early 1960s. The majority of student efforts occurred on a national canvass in the fight against racial discrimination and segregation in the United States and primarily in the South. Students traveled south and organized, following the example of civil rights groups such as the National Association for the Advancement of Colored People (NAACP) and the Southern Christian Leadership Conference (SCLC).[12] Mentored and trained by skilled activists and organizers like Ella Baker and Septima Clark, black college students (often working alongside white college students and other students of color) formed groups like SNCC and CORE.[13] Key features of the activism in this period include:

• the sit-in-style protest of the famed Greensboro, North Carolina, sit-ins at a local Woolworth's lunch counter;

8

• Freedom Rides, which were interstate bus rides on public carriers by black and white protesters to challenge segregated transportation;
• the "jail-no-bail" strategy of refusing bail after protest-related arrests, thus crowding holding facilities and burdening law enforcement agencies;
• direct political organizing—for example, the Mississippi Freedom Democratic Party and its pursuit of congressional representation.

The struggles of these organizations resulted in the passage of the Voters Registration Act and the Civil Rights Act of 1964 and the National Voting Rights Act of 1965.[14] Thereafter shifts continued in black student activism when federal legislation and civil rights demands failed to yield significant differences in the daily lives of black Americans. Growing doubts in the efficacy of the nonviolent civil rights movement gave way to a shift toward Black Power ideology, self-determination, and the rise of the Black Panther Party as a key organization.[15] The student activism that emerged during the civil rights struggle and then the Black Power era represented the dawning of visible student political action in this period. The organizations were sometimes integrated but due to internal tensions were often racially separate.

The shift from national campaigning to increased on-campus resistance and activism occurred afterward in the late 1960s and was marked by the 1968 assassination of Martin Luther King Jr. and the unrest that followed. King's assassination would be a major turning point for the University of Pittsburgh, and Campbell and her classmates would begin organizing just as university administrators began to consider the issues of race on campus. In this period students began to make demands specific to university campuses. This latter period of activism is the primary sphere relevant to this study. Major gains were made within the civil rights movement, however; as a result of King's assassination, the students then began to direct their outrage to local injustice and began to make demands on their own college campuses. Overall, the black student movement that followed cannot be separated from the period's struggle for civil rights, Black Power ideology, or the emergence of black studies as an academic discipline.[16] In 1967 San Francisco State University (SFSU) was the site of protest, student organizing, and upheaval, and eventually SFSU became the first four-year institution to have a black studies department.[17] The students of SFSU joined together to form the Black Student Union (BSU), a moniker that spread and would be assumed by students organizing on campuses from the East Coast to the West Coast.[18] In November 1968 the BSU at SFSU staged a strike that lasted for more than four months and resulted in the start of the black studies program.[19] Following SFSU's example, students at other colleges and universities continued to organize and protest both national issues like the war in Vietnam and the issues on their campuses. On April 18, 1969, students at Cornell University armed themselves and took over a university building until the administration conceded to their demands; at the top of their list was an academic department focusing on black studies.[20]

Following these highly visible and sensationalized cases, student demands and protests increased across the United States, as did the rise of new black studies programs. Some programs were the result of student protest and struggle; others were preventative measures to preempt student confrontation and organization.[21] Other programs and departments arose from the vested interests of social players and organizations such as the Ford Foundation, whose support of black studies was a political response attending to the racial problems that remained in the United States following the civil rights movement and the Vietnam War.[22] While black studies programs and departments were but one of the concerns of black student activists, the high-profile examples on campuses like SFSU and Cornell revealed that student protests should be taken seriously, and that with persistence universities would concede to student demands. Accordingly, campus movements remained on the rise among black student activists, continuing in the style and legacy of SNCC and other student groups organizing for civil rights and Black Power.

There are no major studies of the black student movement at the University of Pittsburgh and the unique nature of the struggle on that campus. However, there is the coincidence and continuity that several visiting scholars from SFSU's black studies department dispersed to the East Coast and specifically to the University of Pittsburgh during the dawning of the BAS.[23] The motivations, strategies, and ideologies of Pitt students during the black student movement align squarely with campus movements and activists across the United States during the period. This historical context is central to understanding Bebe Moore Campbell's participation in the BAS at the University of Pittsburgh to the extent that it highlights organizing strategies, trends, and the general consciousness of college students in the period.[24]

The narrative of the BAS at the University of Pittsburgh offers important insight about Bebe Moore Campbell's participation, leadership, and personal development during this period. Interviews and documents confirm that she was among the founding group in the summer of 1968, assisted with the Computer Center takeover, wrote for the *Black Action News*, served on the Political Action Committee, and helped start the group Black Women for Black Men (BWFBM). She also took courses under the tutelage of renowned writer-activist Sonia Sanchez and Jack L. Daniel, University of Pittsburgh Distinguished Professor of Communication. Furthermore, accounts from classmates, friends, faculty, and staff testify to Campbell's leadership traits and character, confirming that she was a consistent presence, although not formally elected to leadership. Some noticed that she began to develop a political consciousness derived from black nationalism and cultural nationalism, but that she was not invested in aggressive posturing or superficial Black Power rhetoric, which became the current trend of the era. She was also interested in the experiences of black female students and the need for social support resources on campus. During this time Campbell rejected female subordination that accompanied nationalism, and began to write about gender relations between black women and men during her time as a student.

The BAS was founded as a campus-based political group, rooted in the social movement ethos of that generation.[25] It is distinguished from many black student unions because of its strategic, inclusive, nonviolent, and successful approach in crafting a long-standing legacy of African American presence at the University of Pittsburgh. The BAS had its formal start on May 19, 1968, which is also the birthday of Malcolm X. Campbell had just completed her first year at Pitt and was known among peers for her academic excellence.[26] At this time, a group of students that included Campbell gathered during the summer session and issued a list of concerns and demands to be addressed by the administrative leaders of the university.[27] They immediately launched a campaign to increase the awareness of racist issues using campus newspapers, flyers, and public memos addressed to university administrators. Like other student groups of the time, the BAS was concerned with black student admission and support services, the hiring of black faculty, and culturally relevant curriculum changes in the form of a black studies program. Also, just after it formed the group began to provide social and academic support for newly admitted black students on the predominantly white campus.[28] In the fall of 1968 the BAS offered tutoring, special programs, lectures, and workshops that brought African American artists, speakers, activists, and intellectuals to Pitt. In addition to the cultural transformation on campus, the BAS participated in local and national political campaigns with its own protests and statements of solidarity.[29] Initially, the demands were well received by the university chancellor, but they were not implemented in a timely fashion. These delays would ultimately result in the Computer Center takeover of January 1969. For Campbell, the social movement that ensued around her would heavily influence her racial consciousness, and she would intently commit herself to the cause of racial equality, human dignity, and equal access to educational access, social support, and opportunity for black students on her college campus.

As an undergrad, Campbell majored in early childhood education and worked a short stint as a preschool teacher at the Pittsburgh Childhood Environmental Center (a school established by Pitt's Department of Black Community Education, Research and

Development). Barbara Hayden, the director of the Pittsburgh Childhood Environmental Center, shares that Campbell was "a hard-working person; fun—she had kind of a light spirit with the kids . . . free spirit, free thinking, a lot of energy."[30] Thus Campbell valued education as a tool of liberation and volunteered within the BAS to tutor incoming students and tutored school-age children in the Pittsburgh area. As a founding and active member of the BAS and its Political Action Committee, we can observe Campbell's value for active participation in structural and systemic changes that also emerges in her personal activism years later. While Linda Wharton Boyd teases that the Political Action Committee was "a little Black Panther party on campus," she also notes Campbell's general trait of leadership:

> Well she was definitely a leader, she was a leader. And the reason why she was a leader was because she could quickly size a situation, define it, and come up with solutions for resolving it. I mean she could quickly do that. It was her humor that allowed her to do that. She could do that easily. I think she also exhibited . . . she had a keen ear for listening to what was not said . . . to really get at what you wanted to say. She was very good at that.[31]

3M Scholars/University Community Education Program (UCEP) director and BAS mentor Luddy Hayden remembers Campbell as a part of a larger cadre of excellent students and states, "Well Bebe was one of those students that was animated, passionate about the condition of African Americans on that campus and generally."[32] Both male and female classmates respected her participation in the BAS, and she functioned as an example and inspiration to others. She served in multiple capacities and was not limited to clerical work and support roles. Daniel remembers Bebe, who was petite in stature, as resembling a "little tiny 'mighty' like Kathleen Cleaver" and "one of the first females to be a part of the essentially male Political Action Committee."[33] Ultimately, despite the masculinist nature of the black student movement, overflowing from Black Power and black nationalist ideologies,[34] Campbell was able to lead and support the BAS's campus efforts and navigate this period as a young female student with her identity and values intact.

In *How Long, How Long*, Belinda Robnett's analysis of "who does what . . . and why" in a gender-integrated movement, Robnett considers the interplay of race, class, and gender to account for different movement experiences. She contends that "gender hierarchy shaped the structure of the civil rights movement and defined the nature of activist participation."[35] Robnett's study makes the distinction that black women in the civil rights movement were not just organizers but "bridge leaders" within a social movement's "intermediate layers of leadership." She coins the term "bridge leader" to identify those who maintain connections between various constituencies and a social movement or cause.[36] She offers that bridge leaders "cross boundaries between the public life of an organization and the private spheres of its adherents and constituents" and "cross boundaries between personal lives and the political life of the organization," moving primarily in free spaces not controlled by formal leaders.[37] During her time at the University of Pittsburgh, Campbell functioned as a bridge leader within the BAS.

Campbell's activities and roles within the BAS suggest a firm interest in practical and applied manifestations of the Black Power and black liberation theories that fueled the black student movement. Political Action Committee chair Tony Fountain remembers Campbell's various roles in the BAS: "Bebe contributed a number of articles to the *Black Action News* and her talent for writing was quickly evolving and being recognized. . . . She was very opinionated and outspoken in meetings on issues that she had a passion for." Fountain also recalls that although Campbell did not have an official title or elected office within the BAS, she held a strong role in leadership activities within the group: "So she was involved on several fronts. And when we had, I'll call them strategy sessions, she was there. A very strong active participant. It's almost like one of those . . . a chairperson at-large, if you will."[38] The Political Action Committee—whose members donned the black leather attire, Afros, and frowns of the period's Black Power aesthetic—moved beyond the motif and appearance of Black Power and endeavored strategic, assertive, persistent, and diplomatic action to shift the university culture and policy for black students. Although this diplomacy is not usually highlighted in the narrative of black student activism at Pitt or elsewhere, the historical record of the BAS's activities and events at Pitt makes clear that confrontation and violence on the campus were at a minimum and rhetorical threats were not actualized. Furthermore, because of the students' persistence and effective demonstration and negotiation, BAS actions more often than not resulted in acquiescence, compromise, and cooperation from administrators. This sort of thoughtful and diplomatic approach, matched with deliberate, impassioned action, would become characteristic of Campbell throughout her life work and activism.

Fountain's description of Campbell indicates Robnett's concept of the "bridge leadership" that was characteristic of black women activists of the period.[39] Campbell's role as a participant is informal, and she is active on a nonhierarchal strategizing committee. Thus her leadership is embedded in her student activities and is integral to the success of the organization and its efficacy. During the period she may have been unlikely to hold an elected position or formal title, but this does not diminish her role as an important leader in the BAS.

Campbell honed her own bridge leadership traits among this cadre of intelligent and visionary black collegians. Bridge leaders are the people who may not seek or accept the credit but "keep things going"; they maintain the inspiration and momentum in the face of challenges and setbacks.

Throughout her political, academic, and social involvement on campus with the BAS, Campbell demonstrated the personal characteristics that made her stand out. Several accounts by classmates, colleagues, and instructors speak to the nature of her integrity, personality, intellect, and leadership. Because of the BAS's demands, Marita Harper was hired as first librarian in charge of the Hilman Library African American Collection.[40] She remembers Campbell visiting the collection, saying, "Bebe was a very inquiring person, inquisitive rather. . . . And she became a friendly student that I would talk to whenever she was here in the library."[41] Linda Wharton Boyd, who participated in the BWFBM and its study group, shares that "Bebe was bright. Very, very smart. We did a lot of work together. We spent a lot of time working and in the library."[42]

The fall semester of 1968 Campbell and a small circle of returning black students welcomed fifty newly admitted black students to the University of Pittsburgh. This was the largest incoming enrollment of African American students and a first for the university. The new black students were assigned to the Project A program, named to indicate its place as a top priority. Because this was a first for the university, Project A provided new students with academic tutoring and remediation, social support, and transition services. At the time, Campbell was a high-performing sophomore student who entered Pitt through the regular admissions process a year earlier. Because of her stellar academic performance, she was assigned as a regular tutor for Project A students.[43] As a mentor and tutor to new students, Campbell was positioned to recruit new students and advance the agenda of the preliminary BAS planning meeting of the previous summer. Drawing on her interpersonal interactions and dynamic relational style, she was well positioned to become a campus bridge leader. Her personality and leadership style established her reputation for being personable, reflective, and admired by her peers. This allowed Campbell to engage in *frame bridging* (providing information to those most likely to be interested in a social cause) on behalf of the BAS.[44] Thus, in her formal and social interactions with Project A participants and new black students at Pitt, Campbell would be able to support students and inform them of the BAS programs and goals. Utilizing the frame-bridging practice, she would be able to mobilize a constituency to support future BAS actions to improve conditions for black students, faculty, and staff.

Project A was designed to attract students of color and offered modified admission criteria and course requirements for new admits to account for educational disparities and racial discrimination. This program was housed under the auspices of UCEP, another BAS initiative. Linda Wharton Boyd, who entered the

University of Pittsburgh a year later, in 1969, excitedly tells of her rich experience within this program.

> Unlike Bebe I came in under a special program for minority students. . . . Right after I graduated from high school I went to the University of Pittsburgh. I think I was out of school for about three days and then I went to Pittsburgh. I went in the summertime. It was wonderful because I got nine credits. So when everybody got there in August I had nine credits under my belt. We would take trips to New York which I would never forget like the National Black Theatre. . . . They exposed us to so much of the movement. So coming fresh out of high school it was like WOW this is great! I reflect on that period a lot on what Leroi Jones used to say, "If the beautiful see themselves, they will know themselves" and I sorta live by that principle.[45]

To provide a glimpse of the rich cultural programming organized to recognize black culture on campus, Wharton Boyd also recites the long list of notable black figures of the period who were at Pitt as speakers, guests, and visiting lecturers or artists-in-residence. Students were introduced to the likes of Maulana Karenga, Nikki Giovanni, Rob Penny, August Wilson, Sonia Sanchez, Sekou Toure, Don L. Lee (Haki Madhabuti), Leroi Jones (Amiri Baraka), Barbara Ann Teer, and H. Rap Brown.[46] This roster of speakers and visiting teachers helped to characterize and establish a particular discourse that grounded the black students in Black Power and Black Arts movement ideology.[47]

At the University of Pittsburgh, students also participated and performed with the Pittsburgh Black Theatre network as well as the Kuntu Repertory Theatre and black dance ensembles on campus. For the black students, the immersion in Black Power and Black Arts movement ideology was inevitable given the new black studies program and the myriad visitors and artists-in-residence at the university that came with the birth of the BAS. Campbell's involvement as a tutor and "ambassador" for newly admitted students provided necessary and priceless support for black students on the predominantly white campus. Her commitment, presence, and concern reflect key aspects of bridge leadership and serve as a foundation for the second stage of the framing process, *frame amplification* of the BAS agenda for changes on campus.

By 1969 the UCEP had been renamed the Malcolm, Martin, and Marcus Scholars Program, also known as 3M.[48] Luddy Hayden, a BAS mentor, Pitt alumnus, and member of the black studies staff, served as the first director of the 3M Scholars Program and was also associate director of the UCEP. While the UCEP and 3M Scholars programs were firmly in place that fall of 1968, many matters and concerns articulated in the students' demands went unaddressed.

The BAS marked its formal beginning by issuing a clear set of demands to the university administration. Students met formally, developed organizational structures, and strategized on the handling of their demands.[49] There were five core items included in student demands. The first was acknowledgment as a campus organization, receiving budget appropriations, and an office in the Student Union building on campus. Two of the demands addressed BAS involvement in all matters affecting black students on campus. Specifically, the BAS wanted to approve all news and publicity affecting black students and to give input on any university programs impacting this constituency. Regarding student admission and enrollment, the BAS demands included the right to participate in planning the orientation for the fifty incoming black students who would eventually be a part of the Project A program and ultimately the 3M Scholars Program. Within this demand they also insisted on the removal of negative mislabeling for these newly admitted students (that is, "culturally disadvantaged," "at risk"). The major demand that immediately followed the first demand of organizational status focused on increasing black student enrollment each year toward the goal of 20 percent of the student population.

This demand was the most detailed and proposed multiple avenues to achieve this goal. The demands were issued and delivered by the BAS Political Action Committee, of which Campbell was a prominent member. Campbell and her colleagues strategized to formulate a list of demands that explicitly proposed a new collection in the library on African American history and culture, with a black librarian to be hired immediately in the fall of 1968; a black studies program with departmental status and black faculty; increased hiring of black faculty and the promotion of existing ones and student participation in the candidate selection process; a black recruiting team focused on increasing black enrollment; and curriculum shifts that offered a more meaningful and accurate treatment of black and African history.[50]

The university appeared accepting of the demands,[51] and the BAS members continued forward, preparing and organizing for the new black students, planning cultural events on campus and in the community, and developing a wide range of programs for the fall semester of 1968.

The administrative response to the BAS's presence, their demands, and the cultural campus programming ranged from support to benign neglect. For example, black faculty and administrators were overwhelmingly supportive. Luddy Hayden, who held various administrative and instructional positions at Pitt, worked closely with BAS students. Hayden was also assistant dean of students at the time. During this period, the unity of African Americans who were students, campus employees, and faculty, and even local community members, made the BAS even more effective. He recalled that "the community of African Americans on campus at that time was small enough and close enough that there were not distinctions made between people on the basis of what their positions were."[52] Other faculty members became comrades, mentors, and professors for Campbell and the growing black student body. In particular, Jack Daniel and Curtis Porter served as student advisers and were central to the BAS organizing and would later develop the prospectus and curriculum for the proposed black studies program.[53] In 1969 Daniel and Porter became the first cochairpersons of the black studies program, which was named the Department of Black Community Education, Research and Development (DBCERD). Other black faculty addressed the Faculty Senate regarding racism at Pitt[54] and advocated recruiting more black students at the graduate level.[55] One black administrator intervened in the harassment of a black recruitment officer by a white administrator.[56]

The response from white administrators was mixed and markedly different from the involvement of black faculty and administrators. Chancellor Wesley Posvar, for all intents and purposes, agreed to support the issues indicated in BAS demands but did not follow through with meaningful implementation of these changes (thus resulting in the Computer Center occupation in January 1969).[57] A few people were strongly opposed to and threatened by the BAS, as evidenced through fearful letters of concern and continual disparagement and critique of the student group.[58] However, far more white administrators played the middle ground, posing as reasonable, cooperative liberals.[59] They formed study groups and commissions to examine the race problem and paid lip service to gradual and reasonable changes to the university structure.[60] As a result, progress was often delayed, blocked, and thwarted by the bureaucratic process. Students responded to this regularly and intently.[61]

Amid Campbell's active involvement in campus politics and activities, she also began to explore the craft of writing in various capacities. During that time, her writing focused on audiences in her African American communities. Early on, she attempted to write vivid and informative pieces that affirmed identity and healthy social relationships, and exposed political injustice. Campbell's classmate and lifelong friend Linda Wharton Boyd notes her early experiments with writing:

> She was very sure, more than anything she was sure about writing and her writing when we were in college. We took a class, a writing class, I think with Sonia Sanchez. And one thing she taught us was to use all of our senses. I remember she did some popcorn and brought that popcorn in the classroom and you know how you smell cooked popcorn and we had to describe that popcorn and use all of our senses. And Bebe wrote the most beautiful piece about the popcorn! I said, "Wow, how did you come up with that?" But she compared that popcorn to life and what was happening with black people and integration and the burnt kernel compared to the kernel that wasn't fully burnt. It was such a great piece.[62]

As Campbell became a staff writer for the *Black Action News*[63] and actively honed her writing ability in her black studies courses,[64] she began to utilize creative writing and journalism as a way to inform, inspire, and empower black communities. This practice would guide the trajectory of her career in years to come. However, contemporaneous to her enrollment at Pitt, Campbell's writing for the *Black Action News* is one aspect of her bridge leadership and engages in *frame amplification*. As a bridge leader she used her writing to elaborate on the values and beliefs associated with social justice issues on campus and around the world. Her writing and her personal connection to the student body worked together to connect and align individuals' personal concerns, and encouraged them to be politically active in the social movement around them. As a bridge leader, she built upon her relationships and popularity—and added her writing ability—to highlight national, local, and campus issues via the *Black Action News*. Accordingly, the new students on campus were able to connect their social experiences and challenges on campus to the work of the BAS, resulting in an enthusiastic and supportive constituency that would be central for collective action and on-campus protests and demonstrations.

While on campus, Campbell also wrote an essay for a two-entry[65] BAS publication titled *Black Students Seize the Power to Define*.[66] Campbell's essay, "Black Womanhood Defined," seemingly aligns with the patriarchal gender paradigms of the period, placing black women in support of black men. She writes that black women are peers to black men, but seems to protect male ego and perpetuate stereotypes of black women by suggesting that a supportive black woman doesn't question a black man in public or seek to humiliate him. (This is interesting in contrast to observations that Campbell was a diplomatic but vocal and questioning member of the BAS Political Action Committee.) The essay waxes poetic about male-female heterosexual relationships as a site of interdependence, but *does* clearly define black womanhood in terms of equality and mutuality. The focus on support and cooperation with black men also implies the notion that black men have especially suffered hardship during this era. Over-all, she does not openly critique black male patriarchy, nor does she depart from the masculinist script when she suggests that a woman "should not tear her man down" and when she identifies motherhood as "a most essential quality of womanhood." Still, in other places she quotes Nina Simone's "Four Women" and writes, "Black women have toiled just as much as black men have." She also included an empowered understanding in this passage:

> Black womanhood is not walking behind your man, or in front of him, but by his side. That is to say, a black woman worthy of the name would not land her man in public or in front of his friend. She would be cool and wait until they were alone before anything was discussed. Also, this same black woman would demand the same treatment from her man. Like Aretha says, "Respect" is a beautiful concept that must be put into practice between black women and black men. A true black woman should not cringe at the glance of her husband, but be able to deal with a man without fear. She should not allow herself to be demeaned just because she is a woman.[67]

While her writing on race and gender would evolve and mature with time, in this early essay Campbell offers a veiled critique and commentary that emphasizes respect for women and the rejection of public humiliation, devaluation, and violence against women. At the same time, she challenges the notion of black women as subordinate, but still situates them as most valuable in families and relationships with black men. These variations allude to development and formation of Campbell's antisexist politics. This is important because this sort of challenge to patriarchy has been buried in popular accounts of the black liberation era and because it establishes early Campbell's willingness to take on essential and risky topics as a writer.

Campbell's student publication characterizes the third stage of the framing process, *frame extension* (broadening the focus to incorporate concerns not originally a part of the cause). Progressive gender politics were neither central nor secondary to the BAS's campus agenda. In many cases such views were actually antithetical to conservative, masculinist black nationalist discourse. Therefore these young women on campus add to and extend the "frame" or focus of BAS constituents by posing alternative discourse about gender roles. Campbell and Carson make such considerations important to the general goal of liberation and racial equality.

While Campbell, an education major at the time, would take many turns before committing to a full-time career as a writer, we see that she began to explore and hone her writing early on, as a young adult. More important, her writing in this period—while expository rather than fiction—evidences that she embraced writing as a tool for reaching communities and promoting social change, political commentary, and exploring social relationships.

By January 1969, when the status of the BAS demands was still pending, the students took direct and deliberate action. Several of their most urgent demands had been ignored, and students in the BAS decided it was time to take things into their own hands and occupied the central Computer Center building.[68] Campbell was present during the pivotal Computer Center takeover, orchestrated by BAS's Political Action Committee, and she helped rally students to walk out of their classes in protest. Her rapport with classmates and her academic and social capital as a popular, confident, and high-achieving student was key in garnering participation for the student walkout that would precipitate an important standoff between the BAS and the university. Joe McCormick, the BAS's second president, was among the leaders of this demonstration. Hayden, who was also a mentor to McCormick, recalled the nature of the students in the BAS at the time of the takeover:

> One of the things that will always impress me is that they were able to bring the kind of passion and energy to improving their condition on the campus but also to making a difference for those who would follow them, at the same time they were negotiating the academic environment of the university which is what brought them there in the first place. And I'm always cognizant of that and I reflect upon it because many of them knew that as they advocated for change they were

running the risk of jeopardizing the goals and objectives for which they had come to the U of P. When those students decided to occupy the Computer Center they knew that they were placing their futures on the line but they yet did that. And what that speaks to is the seriousness both real and perceived of black people in the country at that time, with conditions at University of Pittsburgh being a microcosm.[69]

On January 15, 1969, students from the BAS entered classrooms in small groups urging that classes be dismissed or that students dismiss themselves to commemorate the birthday of Martin Luther King Jr.[70]

Earlier that day Campbell and her BAS comrades, in a group of about sixty black students, demonstrated at the office of the university chancellor, Wesley Posvar. Students played drums and waited from noon until about 3 p.m., when the chancellor returned to his office. The students confronted Posvar about the lack of progress with their demands and proposed that classes be canceled to commemorate the birthday of the fallen civil rights leader. Posvar expressed his own concern about the "slow progress" on the demands, and though refusing to cancel classes, allowed students to be officially excused if they opted not to attend classes.[71] Campbell was one of the members of the Political Action Committee responsible for canvassing the campus and announcing the protest effort. BAS member Francine Outen Greer also recalled Campbell among the students who entered and interrupted regularly scheduled classes on the day of the takeover:

> Our first action was to get the university to cancel classes for Martin Luther King's birthday. And of course the university said, "We're not doing that," until we went around and went to every classroom and said, "Today is Martin Luther King's birthday. We'd like for you to release your class." Some did, some didn't. So she [Bebe] was involved in that.[72]

Later that day, according to a student newspaper account, there were three small fires set in a central campus building. The fires were put out, and some evening classes had to be canceled.

By 9 p.m. about thirty black students had entered the Computer Center on the eighth floor of the Cathedral of Learning building for a lock-in that would last for more than seven hours. Students reasoned that the Computer Center was central to administrative functioning and thus a vulnerable site of important university information. University police and over a dozen city police officers were on the scene of the takeover. The BAS members refused communication for several hours before releasing a statement. Local community members brought food and blankets showing their support for the students. After five hours of negotiating with security and administrators, an agreement was finally reached.[73] Ultimately, the chancellor acquiesced to redressing the demands that had been neglected.[74]

Pat Clark, one of the few black computer science students invited to the Computer Center action, remembers the students' accomplishment with pride:

> We went and we sat, I remember we sat in there, sat on the floor and certain demands were met. And um I don't know how many hours we were in there. We were in there for quite a time, but it was such a . . . you know, it put the administration in such a nervous point that they actually gave us what we wanted before. . . . All their information was in there, and I don't remember how we got into that main room but we got in there. And we got our demands . . . just about everything that they had requested.[75]

Although students were influenced by the Black Power rhetoric of the period, this was most often manifest through the use of aggressive posturing and language. In some ways, the activities of black students at Pittsburgh align with Bradley's account of black student activism at Columbia and demonstrations at other universities around the nation.[76] Still, no one took up arms, and no violent threats were made during the Computer Center takeover (or during other BAS actions on campus); with the help of black computer science and engineering students, they effectively intercepted the campus mainframe—an important center of campus information and operation. Thus the BAS engaged in nonviolent and strategic protest, and their demands were ultimately conceded. Beyond their core demands, the Computer Center standoff resulted in a flurry of progressive activity, continued struggle, and transformation of the University of Pittsburgh community. This highly successful and nonviolent strategic action is noteworthy and can be attributed to the broad network of support and advisement within and beyond the campus.

Pat Clark, one of the computer science students at the Computer Center takeover, remained close with Bebe throughout her life and describes her friend as "very articulate. She was very outgoing. A lot of people respected her. She got a lot of respect from everybody. Probably because she was pretty and intelligent, and she had purpose. And she had a passion for everything that she did."[77] One of her best friends, Francine Outen Greer, explains her interaction with others:

> She just was always respected for her intellect and her thought processes, and seriousness of purpose, and she could relate to wide spectrums of people, as indicated by some of her associations and friends. There wasn't a certain type of person; if you were interesting, she liked you. Maybe she didn't like you, but she was interested in finding out more about you. . . . And so, she was always open to new experiences, to new people, new ideas. And that's what I like about her, because she might open a door that I might want to go through.[78]

Greer also remarks on Campbell's approach to new experiences and problem solving. She recalls Campbell taking advantage of new opportunities and travel, as well as being a good planner. From college through adulthood, Greer recognizes this pattern as a consistent, lifelong way of being that distinguishes Campbell as a bridge leader.

> If there was something she wanted to do, she could say, "You know what? I'm thinking about doing this." And then she would make it happen. She would ask the right questions, talk to the right people, followed through, and that whole way of functioning I think was very

evident at Pitt. *How do we make this better? How do we make this happen? And she'd figure out a way to make it happen.*[79]

These accounts help to illustrate Campbell's dynamic and bold presence in the activities and decision making of the BAS, particularly the Political Action Committee, which organized the Computer Center takeover. She and many of her contemporaries functioned as bridge leaders who ushered forth an effective action and win for the BAS.

Through her roles as a founding member, tutor, Political Action Committee member, and cofounder of BWFBM, Campbell demonstrates influence in free spaces within the BAS and Pitt's black student community despite the fact that she did not hold a titled or formal leadership role.[80] But specific to the Computer Center action, Campbell's role as bridge leader is evident: she is a member of the Political Action Committee that planned strategic action for the BAS; she personally joins the students who enter classes and call for a walkout earlier on the day of the Computer Center occupation; and she has already engaged in the framing process, bridging new students to the BAS, amplifying their educational goals to becoming politicized campus citizens, and extending their view of black male and female students working alongside one another for the cause of black liberation. As a BAS bridge leader, Bebe Moore Campbell utilized her personality, her popularity, and the power of the pen to strengthen the effort for the student demands on Pitt's campus.

Beyond her roles with the Political Action Committee, as a staff writer for the *Black Action News*, and as a tutor, accounts of Bebe Moore Campbell's participation in the BAS frequently associate her with an all-female subgroup of the organization, BWFBM. The group was first noted for focusing on the tensions of interracial dating between black male students and white female students. Linda Wharton Boyd joined BWFBM and remembered Campbell and the impetus for the group: "She believed in women, she always had this thing about helping women."[81] While the group may have been perceived as frivolous at the time, there is much more to be understood about this collective. Classmates and instructors remember that this group, whose title implies a focus on men and dating, was more accurately a personal development group. The young collegians would meet in the dormitories at night to discuss a variety of topics. The group also studied together and went to the library to meet and work. Whether or not the young women recognized it as such, this sort of purposeful "woman-gathering" is very much a part of the consciousness-raising tradition of the black feminist movement.

What began as an attempt to "help out the brothers, 'cause the brothers need our help,"[82] evolved to self-actualization and female empowerment. The group members embodied black feminist priorities as they created nonhierarchical, all-female "talk-spaces"; addressed issues of self-worth, image, esteem, and integrity among black female students; and countered the black nationalist tendency to view black women as subordinate helpers and sex objects during the period. Sonia Sanchez, who remembers discussion of their group in her course "The Black Woman," no doubt influenced the female students. Sanchez remarked on the pain and difficulty that she found among students who beforehand had no forum for meaningfully engaging gender and race.[83] Joe McCormick, former BAS chairperson, offers the evolution of his perception of Campbell and the BWFBM:

> My recollection of that organization is one of, well let's put it this way, as a young person I looked at it in a very humorous sort of way. In retrospect, I've tried to make some sense out of it in terms of where people's heads were at that particular time. As I recall, . . . one of the incidents that gave rise to the establishment Black Women for Black Men were a couple of the black athletes dating white women [chuckles]. . . . This is the forward edge of womanism in which we have a case of black women defining themselves as black women and all that went along with that. That just occurred to me just this minute. If you had asked somebody in 1968 who was Audre Lorde, we would've said, "Who in the hell you talkin bout? We don't know nothing bout dat." But when you stop and think about [it] . . . the black side of Third Wave Feminism "slash" womanism.[84]

McCormick's reflection is multilayered. As one of the prominent male leaders on campus, he acknowledges not taking the group very seriously at the time. Yet he recognizes in hindsight the significance of the BAS subgroup and the value of its gender-based priorities. McCormick even articulates the antisexist agenda of and the intersectional focus of race and gender associated with the black feminist contributions of third wave feminism.[85] Ultimately, the practice of woman-centered gathering among the young black women on campus had antisexist implications, and the young women actively embodied the burgeoning feminist movements of the late 1960s and 1970s.[86]

It is clear that through multiple vehicles, writing, and membership in BWFBM, Campbell and the young black women on campus were exploring their own ideas and displeasure relative to gender and sexuality between black men and women. Campbell's professor and mentor, Daniel observed that she was conscious of the gendered scripts of Black Power and black nationalism but rejected inferiority or manipulation. He suggests that as a student, she embraced sympathetic support for black men and perceived their experiences with racism as distinct from that of black women's experiences.[87] Campbell exuded a self-worth and confidence that countered subservient scripts for black women. According to her memoir, she departed for college with candid wisdom from her extended community of parents about sex and relationships, and arrived at the University of Pittsburgh with a mature and grounded sense of her womanhood.[88]

Black feminist discourse offers an important critique of the sexual politics of black nationalism, particularly positioning black and white women as sexual objects. Black female intellectuals and activists of the period often engaged these tensions.[89] Accordingly, even as young students Campbell and her cohort of sisters in BWFBM were cognizant of such black sexual politics and organized in their own interests alongside their commitment to black campus activism. In another instance of *frame extension*, their politicization around race becomes a political awareness about the intersection of race and gender dynamics on a college campus and within a social movement. This group functions within the BAS and reveals distinct and differential needs for black female students within a black nationalist–inspired movement organized with hierarchical gender roles. The concerns of these young women about black male students dating white women could have been potentially divisive. Ultimately, the formation of BWFBM mobilized the young black women on campus, preventing a decline in their support and involvement in the BAS.

Campbell and many of her peers from the BAS remained closely tied to the university after they graduated. The Bebe Moore Campbell Scholarship Fund was named for her role as distinguished alumna and university trustee. An important distinction of the black student activism at Pitt is the longevity of the BAS's presence on Pitt's campus and the impact of a strong body of active black alumni. At many institutions, black student unions and activism tapered off over the years. In some cases this was because black studies programs were collapsed or discontinued, and in other cases increased integration and social gains resulted in the de-politicization of black students. To some extent, such de-politicization occurred at Pitt as the student organization shifted and reshaped with the passage of time and the influx and outflow of the student body. During some periods the BAS was less active, and at other times the group focused primarily on social activities and programming. However, the annual Black Week event was sustained for many years after its 1968 inception, and cultural programming continued, as did efforts to increase black enrollment. In October 2009 the African American Alumni Council of the Pitt Alumni Association sponsored the Sankofa Homecoming Weekend. The event theme, "40 Years of Pride Progress and Partnership with the University of Pittsburgh," gathered the African American alumni who were enrolled during the 1968 birth of the BAS. The program booklet documented continuous organizational presence by noting BAS elected leadership from 1968 to 2010.[90] The impact of Campbell and her student activist peers in the late 1960s is evidenced by the substantive increase in black student enrollment, improved campus and cultural experiences, and measurable institutional changes that have been made in the interest of black students and sustained over time. Likewise the

history of the BAS has become a part of the University of Pittsburgh's institutional memory.

Jack Daniel offered that there are key elements to account
for the long-standing African American progress and legacy at
Pitt. He indicated the importance of "sustained commitment of
students with a cultural consciousness," the growing number of
scholarships and programs designated for black students, and the
strategic positioning of black professionals in high-level administration positions as key to this success. Regarding the last element,
Daniel explains the importance of committed professionals interested in "seeing social justice done" and is able to offer a long list
of African American deans, directors, provosts, and vice-provosts
with the ability to facilitate diverse hiring and undergraduate and
graduate admissions.[91] These significant shifts from 1969 to 2009
undoubtedly resulted from the outstanding and ongoing commitment of many other black alumni who have been cultivated
during the period of the BAS and the generations to follow. Black
student activism at Pittsburgh, while mirroring some aspects of
other black campus movements, is unique because the legacy produced a tangible increase in black student enrollment and faculty
and administrative hiring that has been sustained over time, and
a strong alumni base that advocates and supports black faculty
and students. The value for African American culture is reflected
in the Hilman Library African American Collection (which was
established after the 1969 demands), the exhibits in the Cathedral
of Learning, the Sankofa African American Alumni Homecoming
Celebration, and a wealth of student life and activities.

A bridge leader is not initially the spokesperson, the figure-
head, or the "face" of an organization, but often works behind
the scenes. Robnett argues that bridge leaders are often out of
the spotlight, not because they lack leadership experience but
because they are excluded by social construct (that is, gender,
sexuality, or gender role performance). Bridge leaders may be formal leaders at the local level, but historically they tended to be
excluded from the formal leadership tier. They occasionally hold
formal leadership positions in an organization but not in the
greater structure of social movement leaders. Bridge leaders often

initiate organizations and do the groundwork, and thus are more visible before an organization is formalized. The practice of bridge leadership is evident in Campbell's example and throughout the BAS, as many important players worked together to advance racial progress on campus.

There were many factors contributing to the success of the BAS. The rapid change and unrest of the 1960s period might have produced a campus climate that was optimal for student demands and a university more likely to respond to student needs. The campus struggles that were occurring across the nation led the way for students at predominantly white institutions like Pitt to wage a less contentious battle with administrators who were eager to minimize conflict and negative publicity. The administrative response ranged from cooperation and support from the university chancellor to ambivalence, fear, intimidation, disapproval, and even dishonesty and undermining when it came to addressing student concerns in a timely fashion and following through with implementation. Although there was a lot of ambivalence in the campus response to BAS, there were overlapping efforts for campus change that benefited the BAS, from black faculty speaking out about racism on campus and pressing for resources and faculty and postdoctoral hires, to the white activist group Students for a Democratic Society (SDS) supporting BAS from a distance. Also, the urban and segregated area surrounding the campus was experiencing a wave of political consciousness and mobilization. Local African Americans were confronting racism throughout the city in work, recreation, and residential areas. This undoubtedly strengthened the students' confidence, strategy, and power in making demands at the university.

The case of the BAS, considered within the scope of black campus movements of the period, is similarly characterized by the typical militant posture and Black Power aesthetic, and boasted very strong alliances with black faculty, staff, and local community members. But also there were many young women and men, like Campbell, who stood in the gaps as bridge leaders—making sure that people stayed connected, that the details were considered, and that the movement kept going. Robnett offers that successful social movements also rely on rational planned activities and organization, and she emphasizes the necessity of political opportunity. She states that "the institution must be open to challenges or the incipient movement would be crushed."[92] It is significant that the students at the University of Pittsburgh were successful in gaining administrative cooperation without violence or the threat of violence (that is, taking up arms). The organized and structured format of the group and its subcommittees proved effective in establishing a voice on campus, issuing demands. The BAS responded to the neglect and the unfulfilled promises, and orchestrated the ultimate acceptance and implementation of their demands following the Computer Center action. Furthermore, the BAS assisted with black student recruitment, orientation, tutoring, and social support through the UCEP. The students also engaged in collaborative efforts with the Hilman Library African American Collection, as well as the black faculty and the black studies department. Accordingly, black student activism at Pittsburgh was successful in fomenting institutionalized shifts and advancements within the university that have been sustained over time.

During her college years at the University of Pittsburgh, Bebe Moore Campbell was genuinely concerned with black culture and identity, and racial and economic inequities. She was swayed by neither the aesthetics of black activism nor the performance of patriarchy and militancy.[93] But the political concerns of race, culture, and identity drawn from black nationalism would inform the thematic concerns that she would revisit throughout her life, in both her writing and activism. She appeared to cultivate her interest in writing and journalism through *Black Action News*; in the black rhetoric course taught by Jack Daniel; and writing with Sonia Sanchez in her class, "The Black Women."[94] These experiences surely nurtured the seeds of racial and social consciousness represented by the multiple and overlapping movements of the period.

Campbell's education, development, and maturation span periods of early civil rights activism, the Black Power and the Black Arts movements, and black women's growing response and engagement in the women's liberation movement. Furthermore, we can draw conclusive information about the overall impact of the BAS on Campbell given her participation and roles in the group (tutor, member of Political Action Committee, staff writer for *Black Action News*, cofounder of BWFBM). We also learn about her as a person, about the intellectual and creative resources that she brought to the BAS, and about her reputation for integrity, compassion, seriousness, intensity, and commitment. There are many implications that her work as a student activist holds for antisexist discourse within black feminist and womanist theories.[95] Campbell occasionally identified as feminist or womanist later in life.[96] Overall, she leaned toward community-focused, culturally grounded, and woman-centered experiences during her years at the University of Pittsburgh.

After graduating from the University of Pittsburgh in 1971 with a degree in early childhood education, Bebe Moore Campbell's life took multiple turns. As an intellectual biography, this book does not highlight all of these directions; however, there are some key events to note. In her early twenties, Campbell spends time traveling abroad to Africa, South America, and Europe.[97] She moves to Atlanta in the 1970s and teaches in the public school system. In 1975 she marries her first husband, Tiko Campbell, at the age of twenty-five.[98] The couple then births a daughter, Maia, in 1976. Campbell begins to think seriously about leaving teaching for a career in writing or business and decides to relocate to Takoma Park, Maryland, near the Washington, DC, metro area. During the 1980s Campbell divorces, experiences the death of her father, and begins to pursue writing through a career in journalism and by taking writing workshops at Howard University.

The career shifts of her young adulthood brought Bebe Moore Campbell certain clarity about her calling as a professional writer. She had cleared the path in many ways, as a corporate writer for AT&T Telephone Company (circa 1978) and then as the Washington, DC, correspondent for *Black Enterprise* magazine (circa 1980). Campbell took advantage of freelance opportunities offered by major newspapers and popular magazines, like *Essence*.[99] She continued to nurture her interest in journalism and was a member of the National Association of Black Journalists, thus adding news and radio commentary to her freelance work. Simultaneously, she committed to honing her craft as a creative writer by participating in writing workshops and classes led by noted black literary giants Toni Cade Bambara and John Oliver Killens. In the 1980s Campbell publishes two nonfiction works. Her major aspiration was to move from editorial and nonfiction writing to creative fiction. In the 1980s Campbell would make two major life shifts: she left her day job behind to launch a full-time commitment to fiction writing, and she relocated from the East Coast to Los Angeles, where she marries her second husband, Ellis Gordon, and establishes herself as prominent novelist and activist.

In the 1990s Campbell's community activism shifts to focus on mental health awareness and equity in black communities. Shifting her early experience as a black student activist, Campbell's social justice work turns to a more personal matter affecting her family. When her daughter, Maia, is diagnosed with bipolar disorder, Campbell takes on mental illness, a long-held taboo in many black communities, and becomes an advocate for improved resources, policies, and public discourse.

Campbell remained an active supporter of her alma mater, was appointed as an alumni trustee, and also was awarded with an honorary doctorate from the university. The influence of her college years and the development of her unique practice of bridge leadership, service, and personal activism can be considered in three ways: Campbell's active role in the BAS, the collaborative formation of the BWFBM, and the development of her interest in writing. The personal characteristics and traits that she brought to her various works on campus would serve as a foundation for lifelong activism and her effective practice as a community bridge leader.

# Private Matters and Public Health: Campbell Takes On Mental Illness at Home and in the Community

*I have a mentally ill family member. And I saw the illness begin to manifest about eight or nine years ago. And at that point I was shut down completely. Went right into denial. Allowed stigma to overtake me. I was ashamed and embarrassed. I didn't want to talk about it. I forbid anyone in the house to talk about it outside of the house.*
—Bebe Moore Campbell, interview by Ashok Gangadean
(*Global Lens*), February, 5, 2006

In the late 1990s, after her daughter, Maia, was diagnosed with mental illness, Bebe Moore Campbell began to take special interest in mental health and its effect on families and communities. This season of activism is marked by Campbell's growing practice of bridge leadership. Many bridge leaders operate in free spaces, making connections that formal leaders cannot, and employ a one-on-one interactive style of leadership for mobilization and recruitment. Individuals who are considered bridge leaders tend to have greater leadership roles in nonhierarchical structures and organizations and may act as formal leaders as needed—for example, in moments of crisis. In general, they are closer to the wishes and desires of the constituency because they do not need the formal legitimation of outside structures or authorities. For this same reason, bridge leaders may advocate more radical and nontraditional tactics. Much like her collegiate involvement in the Black Action Society (BAS) during the 1960s black student movement, Campbell's mental health activism also demonstrates her continued work as a bridge leader.[1]

Campbell's personal life continued to bloom after she relocated to Los Angeles to become a full-time writer. In 1986 she remarried and merged families with Ellis Gordon, a divorced dad and banker. The two remained together for twenty years, through her short battle with cancer and her untimely death in 2006. By the late 1990s Campbell's market success and the reception of *Your Blues Ain't Like Mine* positioned her as a bona fide novelist. She received critical acclaim, book awards, and national recognition on her relevant and exacting depiction of the racial fabric of the nation. Now living in Los Angeles, Campbell would follow *Your Blues* with three more novels over the course of a decade. In each work she utilized and expanded many of the style techniques, themes, and literary devices found in *Your Blues*.[2] During this time she would also become involved in mental health activism.

Ellis Gordon's recollection of his courtship and early relationship with Bebe Moore Campbell offers much about understanding her personality, convictions, and future work with the National Alliance on Mental Illness (NAMI). Gordon describes his wife's value for her family, for healthy relationships, and for emotional and physical wellness. This was especially evident by her insistence on counseling before and during their marriage. Her husband recollects that

> she was big into counseling, so I said, "Well, eh . . . I'll go to some counseling." . . . So I anticipated the counseling—we would go two or three times and that would be it. Maybe two or three weeks, that's it [chuckles]. Six months later, we're still in counseling. The good news about the counseling for us is that our backgrounds are totally separate—but our core values were the same. And that was what we discovered during the course of the counseling. So it just worked out to be a really good counseling session and it went, like I said on for six months. And it really formed a firm foundation for our relationship. So I was able to convince her to marry me November 10 of 1984.[3]

Gordon went on to explain that they later joined a group of couples who met to strengthen and nurture marital bonds and featured an annual retreat with a marriage professional. He describes Campbell's "penchant for counseling,"[4] which also evidences her interest in emotional health, self-improvement, and support in cooperative group settings. This "penchant" is reminiscent of the self-help and mutual support group she cofounded with other black female students during her college years. In the years preceding her activism with NAMI, Campbell cultivated very strong marital, familial, and filial bonds. These relationships would prove to be a critical support mechanism for Campbell in years to come.

The late 1990s would bring Campbell face-to-face with the formidable experience of having a loved one diagnosed with mental illness. Although she never compromised the privacy of her relative, after Campbell's death it became apparent and public that she was referring to her adult daughter, Maia, who was a popular sitcom actress in the 1990s. Initially, Campbell grappled with this privately with her family for some time before turning a corner and sharing her experience with others. Ellis Gordon describes the period following their discovery of their daughter's illness:

> In 1998, that's when we first found out that we had a loved one . . . and at the time the loved one was unnamed, we never said who she was. But that was the turning point in our lives that we had a loved one with mental illness. And it was something that we were totally unequipped to deal with because mental illness was something that you always read about or heard about. It didn't impact you because it was like, "Oh that's unfortunate." But you didn't have a feel for what it really is or how it will impact you. And we found more and more, just based on our own experience and inability to deal with it or to want to deal with it. Not wanting anybody to know.[5]

Maia Campbell guest-starred on several sitcoms in the 1990s but is best known as a regular, playing the role of Tiffany on the sitcom *In the House* starring Debbie Allen and LL Cool J. Maia's celebrity as a television actress made her shifts in her behavior more visible, and yielded major media attention. As she struggled with her illness, the public took notice, often exploiting her because she was young, attractive, and famous. She was accused of prostitution and drug addiction, and suffered hostile depictions by Internet bloggers and gossip sites that spread in a rapid and "viral" fashion. In response to an onslaught of negative social media, a statement from the family published on Essence.com[6] acknowledged Maia's illness, corrected rumors, and expressed appreciation for responsible journalists who did not exploit the matter. Her stepfather, Gordon, shares:

> Well, it's very difficult to keep secrets with a person with mental illness because they usually disclose it themselves. So it's fairly obvious, it's out there now. For all intents and purposes, it's public knowledge. That's why with the letter I attempted to blunt some of the things that was going on. That's why we did the interview with Essence.com and came out with a statement to say that we got her in treatment. But yes, it is Maia, and I think everybody—it's kinda like the worst-kept secret. They kinda knew, but since we didn't have her approval to do it, we didn't want to out her. . . . Well it was in respect for Maia not wanting it to be known, but not fear of saying it . . . but it doesn't take a rocket scientist if you say "a loved one" and there seems to be strange things are going on with your daughter, it doesn't take much to put two and two together.[7]

The experience of this very personal and sometimes painful matter would lead Bebe Moore Campbell into nearly a decade of loving, committed activism and service to individuals and families living with mental illness.

When Campbell first learned of her daughter's diagnosis with bipolar disorder, she experienced the classic stages associated with grief and loss.[8] Along the road to acceptance, feelings of embarrassment and doubt were sure to arise as well. Very close friends and social acquaintances alike recall the moments when she finally revealed her family's secret, or the fact that she did not say anything at all. Joe McCormick, a classmate of Campbell's from the University of Pittsburgh, recalls that although he and his wife were social acquaintances of Campbell's when she lived in the

DC/Maryland area, they did not learn of her trials for some time. He recounts hearing the news from a third party:

> A mutual friend—not an acquaintance—but a mutual friend told me what Bebe was wrestling with . . . and I said "Ohhhhhhhhhhh," because Bebe was simultaneously an open person and a private person. She had both of those parts of her personality. And I am not a person that gets into your business. If you wanna share your business with me I'm there to listen and not judge. Bebe never brought Maia's challenges to Janet and me. We found out about that indirectly.[9]

Linda Wharton Boyd, another college friend who maintained an intimate friendship with Campbell and her family, remembers when she gathered several of her East Coast friends together to tell them her secret all at once. Wharton Boyd states that although she knew a little bit about the situation, it was on that weekend that Campbell fully disclosed to her friends details of her struggle:

> Now I knew that she was going through some things before, because she had shared some things with me. But [not] the innermost soul of that whole thing. . . . I think we were at her house in Martha's Vineyard the summer before she told the whole group about the loved one and I was like "something is not right here girlfriend, something's not right."[10]

She goes further to describe the courage and intentionality of Campbell's disclosure:

> What stands out to me is that Bebe was never too 'shamed to seek help for situations that she faced or that her friends faced. Now when she got involved in the mental health piece it was because of a loved one who had mental illness and she struggled with that quietly for awhile. Quietly meaning her and her family. But she couldn't keep that from her friends. So she made a trip back east and pulled us all together . . . when she shared what she was going through, and I use the term publicly loosely—not meaning big, big public but public meaning outside of her inner circle and outside of her family. When she was beginning to share that and met up with a group of women who were going

through what she was going through is where she found comfort and strength with what she was going through.[11]

Talking with her East Coast friends into the wee hours of the night was only a step in taking a public stand in the campaign for mental health awareness. Creating dialogue had been a key strategy of Campbell's activism at the University of Pittsburgh. As she gathered old friends, many of whom were Pitt alumni, to share about her daughter, this would be the first of many conversations that would launch her involvement in the mental health movement.

In 2003 five middle-class African American women started a local affiliate chapter of the NAMI, NAMI Urban Los Angeles (NULA). According to primary and secondary accounts,[12] these women first met as an informal support and prayer group, but eventually evolved into something greater than any one of them could have imagined alone. Much like her gathering with classmates to form Black Women for Black Men on the University of Pittsburgh campus in 1968, Campbell joined with these mothers simply to talk with and console one another. Through this prayer group, she continued in a similar pattern of bridge leadership, consciousness raising, and organizing with women. Initiating this act of frame bridging, the first step in framing alignment theory, these mothers joined together the "frames" of their parental concern and their interest in mental health resources. These gatherings would continually expand to birth a full-fledged movement in their community. At first Campbell grappled with the uncertainty that faced her family and kept the matter a private one, even after sharing the diagnosis with her dearest friends. Eventually, she would begin to speak openly about her experiences, both in a public capacity as well as in one-on-one settings, extending compassion and support to women coping with similar situations.[13] Yet full disclosure would be a long road ahead. There would be one instance of disclosure that would set a course of events and spawn the birth of an organization that would aid an entire community.

Nancy Carter, cofounder and executive director of NULA, recalls the challenges of her first efforts to connect with Campbell.

Carter had discovered her son's diagnosis with mental illness in the same time period as Campbell's discovery about her daughter, Maia. Campbell and Carter shared similar social circles but did not actually know one another, so a mutual friend attempted to connect the two women. While both women had support from a few trustworthy friends, in neither case were any of their friends experiencing the act of parenting an adult child with mental illness; nor were they familiar with how to cope with such a life-changing event. According to Carter, Campbell was reluctant to meet, fearing that Carter might "put her business in the street."[14] In her own words, Campbell later shared this fear in an interview with *Black Enterprise* magazine:

> We don't want to talk about it. I didn't want to talk about it, either. I went into denial. I was ashamed. I was very stigmatized by this illness that had no business in my family. But it was. So I had to confront the stigma. And it took me years to come to grips with it and to control the impact it had on my life. And those were years of secrecy and shame.[15]

At this time, Campbell clung to her privacy in fear of the deep social taboo that could tarnish the image of her and her family and position her for undue judgment and critique. Nonetheless, the two of them finally stepped across their avoidance and made arrangements to meet. Carter remembers:

> My son was diagnosed with bipolar disorder in 1994. I was very open about it, because I was a single mom; I needed help. I didn't know where to go. And Bebe didn't want to talk to me. But eventually you get to a point where you gotta reach out to somebody. It just gets too heavy. So I got a phone call one day. And I knew the minute I heard her voice, why she was calling. And so I called her back, we talked a little bit on the phone and I think we were both kinda hesitant with each other. I had never really . . . I didn't have anybody who was walking the same walk I was walking. So we decided to meet.[16]

They met at a Sunday morning church service and actually bonded before many words could be exchanged. Carter recounts:

We agreed to meet there for Sunday service and we did. And she came with Ellis and I was by myself and we decided we would go to church and then I would go back over to her house after the service was over, you know, we'd talk. And I can't remember the song or what was happening in the service but there was a moment in time when we just both reached for each other's hand and we were holding on for dear life and crying our eyes out. And you know, you just can't explain it, it's that thing that happens when you're in the deep end of the pool and somebody else is too. So that's where it started.[17]

They shared their respective accounts of the hardships, frustrations, and hurts that mental illness had brought to their lives. Realizing they were not alone in this experience brought about catharsis and a glimpse of healing for the two mothers—a healing that they wanted to share with others. Carter reasoned to Campbell that there had to be other parents out there experiencing the same struggle and feeling alone. She describes the moment the idea popped in her head to start a group, and she saw the wheels begin to turn in Campbell's head:

[We] ended up going back to her house and talked about each of our stories and what we were going through and I had always thought that there were other people out there like me and [wondered] how would I get to them. And I said to Bebe, I said, "Look, why don't we start a group?" I said, "I've been thinking that there might be other people, now that I've got you. . . . " And I no sooner got the words out of my mouth, she was like "yeah, I'm there." At that point I didn't know the activist she had been, Honey, she was like "oh yeah, let's do it."[18]

By the time she left Campbell's house, Carter says their new friendship was already "forged in the fire."[19] Similar to her college activism in the BAS, Campbell's bridge leadership emerged with the idea to initiate a formal group. Like many bridge leaders, she would be present for the foundational work and more active and visible prior to the actual formation of an organization.[20]

Eventually, through word of mouth they were able to pass along information about a meeting hosted at Carter's home. At the first meeting a tentative group of strangers and distant acquaintances arrived seeking help, but unsure of what they might find.[21] Among those attending was Dr. Lynn Goodloe, a surgeon, later to become board president of NULA, who had come along with a friend, Jo Helen Graham (also a cofounder). Goodloe was surprised to find herself in the home of Nancy Carter, with whom she was familiar, and even more shocked to see that Bebe Moore Campbell was present, greeting the guests as well. The uncanny coincidence was not only because of the fact that Goodloe recognized Campbell and had shared casual friendship with the writer, but also that their children, Campbell's daughter and Goodloe's son, were schoolmates who had attended their senior prom together. Goodloe recalls her surprise:

> I think it was around '99 or 2000 . . . somewhere in there I got a phone call from another friend, Jo Helen Graham. . . . She called me to come meet over Nancy Carter's house because I think she heard I was having some problems with _____. But anyway, I walked into Nancy's house and who's sitting there but Bebe. And we looked at each other like, "what are you doing here. . . . " You know and then the tale begins with a bunch of . . . we mothers who met originally as a prayer group. So we would meet periodically to pray over our children and our loved ones who were having struggles and it wasn't even clear to us then what was going on.[22]

Recovering from seeing the mother of her son's prom date in the kitchen, Goodloe stayed, and the group began to take shape.[23] Collectively these women commenced the framing process—specifically, the frame-bridging stage—and would begin shifting their collective concern and prayers to a shared interest in gathering information and resources for families coping with mental illness.

The group would meet to pray, share their stories, and discuss their concerns, frustrations, doubts, and issues in coping with mental illness in their child's life. Eventually they realized the need for resources, information, and formal support around brain disease. As the focus began to change, a shared vision would crystallize. This shift indicates the group's movement to _frame amplification_, the stage when a social movement builds momentum based on a pronounced recognition of shared beliefs. The group discussed their concerns about the accessibility of resources for families like their own, and the suggestion came up to research support information online. One person shared that NAMI provided an informational course for families; from there, the trajectory from informal support to forming a nonprofit advocacy group begins. Campbell located the Family-to-Family class, a peer education course offered by NAMI that explores mental illness from diagnosis, characteristics, and treatments to what to expect with loved ones and how to engage the mental health system. Campbell attended this class with her mother, Doris. Feeling empowered and transformed, she returned insisting that the other women take the course, once again exhibiting bridge leadership at the early stages of the organization's founding. Goodloe retells the sequence of events:

> Jo Helen Graham told us it was a course to take . . . the NAMI Family-to-Family course. And she introduced us to that and I think Bebe took it first. And then Nancy Carter and I took it together, and it was everything you ever wanted to know about mental illness from A to Z. So we all took it at different times. So we continued to meet, praying over our kids, and we were a mother's prayer group. And from there we decided we needed to do more than prayer, we needed to be activists. So that's when we cofounded, originally it was NAMI Inglewood, then we changed it to NAMI Urban LA, but it was NAMI Inglewood. And then we also took the teacher training so we could actually teach the Family-to-Family course and help other people. We decided that we definitely, obviously, were always gonna be advocates for our family members with mental illness, but we also felt there was a void in the black community.[24]

As Carter and Goodloe followed Campbell in taking the Family-to-Family course, the three women were invited to take the trainer education course, which would prepare them to teach the Family-to-Family course to others. Whether or not they realized it, the women were expanding their expertise in order to eventually engage a broader constituency of families in need of support.

At this time they had to travel to Beverly Hills and sometimes far outside of the Los Angeles city limits to attend courses in a predominantly white community. They realized that African American families from their community, particularly the poor and working class, would not have the luxury to travel all the way to Beverly Hills to get help for their children with mental health needs. Empowered with new information and teaching tools, this time the women decided to start their own NAMI affiliate. Their one commitment was that they would center their work in an urban community, offering access to support and resources that hitherto was absent in the African American neighborhoods. With this clarity, Campbell and her cohorts move to the third stage of framing—frame extension. Thus there was a fluid transition from sharing concerns and prayers, to seeking information for families in need, to ultimately redelivering resources and support tools to African American communities with pronounced disparities in access. The women began teaching the class locally and agreed soon after to form the nonprofit, which they initially ran out of a converted office in Carter's home. Using rented space, they offered support groups for consumers and families as well as the twelve-week Family-to-Family education course. The founding members, participants of the mothers' prayer group, birthed the local chapter of NULA to serve local black and Latino communities. Goodloe explains:

> There was a lot of denial, a lot of misconception, a lot of stigma, and we felt we really needed to do what we founded our chapter to do which was educate, support, and advocate. Because when you have somebody with mental illness it is a "dark deep by yourself" hole and you think you're the only one on the face of the earth having these unbelievable challenges, but there are a lot of people out there. So we wanted to educate and then we do support group because we want other people to know that they weren't alone and that was part of our slogan "No Family Stands Alone."[25]

This practice of getting people to be aware and involved is a clear example of frame bridging, or connecting people to information about a social issue. Realizing the value of information and community, these mothers formed the NULA affiliate and took on the cause to "educate, support, and advocate" for families and to minimize the negative perceptions that mental illness carries.

In the process of informal support meetings and envisioning the NAMI affiliate group, these women and their families forged intimate bonds as they navigated the unpredictable, sometimes volatile and painful journey through mental illness. It was not uncommon for these friends to aid a family when their loved one was in crisis, went missing, or landed in a jail or mental health facility.[26] As Ellis Gordon describes Campbell's role, he notes that her work with NAMI went beyond fund-raising and conjuring ideas:

> Not only was she a strategist, but she didn't mind getting her hands dirty, and she would get in and do whatever needed to be done, to make sure it got done. Because this was a cause that needed to be heard. . . . I mean many nights she'd come home and she'd be tired. And another thing too was kinda like being a support group for one another. . . . We would get a call in the middle of the night, and we'd have to go rescue somebody. That was a part of it. I mean some nights we'd be sleeping in our sweats if there was something going on. You know, anything to help them or the parent. Or in some cases just being there with the person as support, moral support. Sometimes going to the jail with them or going to the hospital with them, just being there.[27]

The network formed by Campbell, Carter, Goodloe, and the other mothers illustrates key aspects of bridge leadership, partly because of the lack of hierarchy. Each individual's leadership emerged as needed. For example, in these moments of crisis when an adult child went missing, Campbell and the other women moved easily into action and leadership. Campbell tended to prefer these "free spaces" and would later focus less on informational classes and more on the support groups provided by the affiliate chapter. Again, as during her college days, these small groups allowed her to employ "a one-on-one interactive style of leadership" much like the group meetings of BWFBM in the female dorms of the University of Pittsburgh in 1968.[28]

Accordingly, the importance of having support and advocacy with a mentally ill family member cannot be overstated. The families were present for one another to assist not only when a loved one was in crisis and became distressed or confrontational. Other times they stood together in court or at a police department when a judge or law enforcement officer might have been unsympathetic or uninformed about the needs of someone with mental illness. Similarly, they advocated for their children if a health professional or facility staff person offered less than quality information or care. The women also shared triumphs when a loved one was doing well or was compliant to treatment.

Recognizing the weight of this work on both their bodies and their psyches, the founding members of NULA would occasionally treat themselves to a day at the spa in efforts to restore and return to work. Dr. Goodloe comments on the recuperative value that these self-care days held for the quality and continuation of their activism:

> All of us who taught and started our chapter, per what we learned, would get into the self-care too, because you know, you can't help somebody else unless you've got yourself together too. So the self-care part for us was we used to love to go to the spa, so we were affectionately known as SPA-NAMI too. Because when we'd go to court to support people, we'd go down to prison and get them out of jail, we'd go to the sheriff's office. We'd do all this heart and labor intensive, emotional work, and then we'd sit down, take a breath, and go to the spa and chill. So it was a way to restore yourself and get yourself remotivated so you don't drain yourself with this difficult work sometimes, so that was a really fun part we used do.[29]

Little is said in public space about the emotional angst, fear, grief, and distress of parents responsible for an adult child with mental illness. However, considering the toll and the pain that sometimes accompanied their efforts, these nurturing and wellness practices were central to the success of this once-prayer group, turned grassroots-community mental health organization.

NULA, an affiliate site of NAMI, serves the local African American community in South Los Angeles and the broad cause of mental health awareness. Founded in 2003 by Dr. Lynn Goodloe, Bebe Moore Campbell, Jo Helen Graham, Judy Ann Elder, and Nancy Carter, first under the name NAMI Inglewood, this inner-city affiliate would address the need for mental health awareness in an underserved community.[30] The founding board members included Goodloe (president), Carter (vice president), Campbell (treasurer), and Graham, who were joined by Dr. Benita Council (other board members would join later, including Ellis Gordon, who would replace his wife as treasurer after her death).[31] In the same year, Campbell published a children's book, *Sometimes My Mommy Gets Angry*. Utilizing her profession and gift of fictional writing, this book was written with her own granddaughter in mind and offered young children a narrative model of how to cope and safely respond to parents with mental health issues. Campbell also wrote her first play, *Even with the Madness*, which previewed in Los Angeles and debuted in New York City.[32] The play also took on the topic of coping with the mental illness of family members, particularly within African American families. The three central focus areas of the group are to educate, to support, and to advocate.

The women from the mothers' prayer group understood intuitively that African American communities with disparate access to mental health care and resources also faced cultural stigmas and historical barriers to openly addressing mental illness. While the national agenda on mental illness has grown in importance and urgency, the discourse on mental health issues in African American communities requires distinct social, cultural, and historical considerations. Historical moments like the use of enslaved Africans in inhumane medical inquiries[33] and the tragic legacy of the Tuskegee syphilis experiment[34] evidence the impact of racism on medicine and health care and have resulted in long-standing distrust of medical institutions by African Americans. When it comes to mental illness in African Americans, history revealed serious problems in underestimating the occurrence of mental illness, the need for care, differential access to mental health services, and the "social and cultural distance between patient and clinician."[35] Other studies examine the cultural bias, misdiagnosis, and overpathologizing of African Americans with regards to mental health.[36] These issues make mental health a difficult and slippery slope for consumers and families to navigate. The need for mental health awareness and advocacy thus takes on particular significance within African American communities.

Given her political awareness and personal experience, Campbell clearly realized that African Americans have a history of distrust and discord in the legacy of racist and abusive medical care and treatment. The added fear of social stigmas that could yield an even more negative perception of African American individuals and communities poses its own challenge to improving mental health awareness and care. Finally, while the traditional modes of coping and therapy through religious and spiritual counseling often hamper willingness to consider pharmacological and psychological treatment options, there is a shift toward partnerships that promote adequate care. These factors interact with contemporary health disparities and make the campaign to improve African American mental health all the more critical. Overall, the distinct stressors of racism and cultural norms that inhibit the display of vulnerability necessitate such group-specific health care solutions. The current state of the mental health care system begs for increased attention and advocacy on behalf of African American populations.

Campbell and her circle of activist-mothers agreed that a starting point in closing the gap in mental health disparities for African Americans would be the accessibility and accuracy of resources, information, and quality services. While she preferred to work in the support group setting, Campbell was the first of the mothers to seek out and enroll in the educational programs on mental illness. NULA provides "user friendly" content on mental illness in several ways. The Family-to-Family class is a twelve-week course for family members and caregivers of individuals with severe mental illness. The class is provided free of charge and is taught by other family caregivers—hence the name, Family-to-Family. Participants meet for two-and-a-half hours each week and learn comprehensive information about brain disease and treatment options. Nancy Carter, the primary instructor for the course, remembers her first time taking the class:

> It changed our lives, to have so much information, to be in rooms where you see so many other people going through what you're going through and to learn. . . . You know just to learn more about how to handle your loved one, how to . . . what the illnesses really are . . . cause you don't get any information from the hospital and the doctors.[37]

She further explains that

> the classes [are] strictly educational. It will give you some informa-tion about psychosocial, biological aspects of mental illness. Basically I call it the "Everything you wanted to know about Mental Illness, but you never asked anybody or nobody told you." Two-and-a-half hours. Twelve weeks. *By* families, *for* families. And strictly educational.[38]

The affiliate also provides a version of this course in Spanish, although it has not been able to develop broader outreach for Latinos due to funding limitations.

Similarly, the Peer-to-Peer course is a nine-week program not for families but for the "individuals recovering from severe mental illness." This peer-taught course empowers mental health consumers to aid fellow consumers.[39] NULA also sponsors a pro-vider education course in which consumers, family members, and professionals deliver content to mental health service providers. In another NAMI course, "In Living Color," the NULA affiliate instructs primary care physicians who do not specialize in men-tal illness but need to be prepared to recognize, treat, or make referrals for patients who have psychiatric illnesses. In addition to these courses, a new program for law enforcement, "The Color of Justice," educates police and court officers on the unique needs of offenders with mental illness.

Providing adequate support services is another central part of NULA and the lifeblood of the affiliate. Whereas the education classes serve a primarily informational function, the support groups offer assistance with coping, sharing opportunities, and community. Prior to her death, Bebe Moore Campbell took the lead in the support activities of the organization, and this is where she thrived as a bridge leader. Campbell enjoyed facilitating the sharing of stories, the encouragement, the social outings, and the group activities for this arm of the affiliate's programming. The interpersonal and intimate nature of support groups aligns with Campbell's style of bridge leadership such that she was more inclined to work behind the scenes with the needs of the consumers and families. Although her celebrity made her the spokesperson within the national organization, she was more interested in the "wishes and desires of the constituency" than legitimation outside of the local NAMI affiliate.[40]

There are three primary groups for support at NULA.[41] The Family-to-Family support group (distinguished from the informational class of the same name) serves family members of persons with brain disease. The NAMI Connection is designated for anyone living with mental illness and, like the education classes, is peer led. The NULA branch also identified the needs of armed services veterans returning from duty in Iraq and Afghanistan without adequate reentry support and services. According to Carter and Goodloe, veterans would come home and find themselves distressed, uninformed about available resources, and sometimes homeless. Consequently, they added veterans to the body of constituents they would serve. The veteran-specific support group, Veterans of Color Action League (VOCAL), addresses the post-traumatic stress disorder experienced by many servicemen and women. This strand of service has also included a veterans fair during National Minority Mental Health Month and workshops at Veterans Administration (VA) facilities. By providing a wide array of classes, workshops, and support programs, the affiliate serves to break silence, challenge stigma, and promote healthier lives for individuals and families. The services that NULA offers extend beyond meetings and into daily lives with ongoing involvement and assistance. The office would receive multiple calls each day with queries and requests for situational help. Sometimes affiliate members provide resources or even accompany families and individuals as they navigate the mental health and legal system. NULA headquarters and the website provide information such as prescription assistance and a resource guide entitled *What to Do When a Loved One Is Arrested*. According to Dr. Goodloe, this essential document provides

> a step-by-step process of what to do, contacting the jail and making sure they're in the mental health part of the jail and knowing what their medications are. Any problems, if there's a suicide attempt, I mean it's a whole document you fill out, and telephone numbers, hours, visiting hours, it's pretty comprehensive. I think it's on the main NAMI website too, but it's on ours as well.[42]

She also refers to the "unofficial" support and services that the chapter provides its members:

> So, I mean outside of the office it's anything from going to court to support people with loved ones who are going to court, it could be picking somebody up from court, you know going to visit someone in the jails.[43]

This need for extended support to families and consumers informs the multilayered advocacy of NULA. Campbell's close connection with the chapter's support services embodies bridge leadership such that she enjoyed working in an informal capacity and kept a close proximity to the people living with mental illness on a daily basis. Working at this level, Campbell utilized her compassion and empathy to support a healthy lifestyle for consumers and families.

Within the NULA affiliate, the women work as shared leaders offering direct consumer advocacy and resources to its local members. However, the resources, hotlines for crisis and support, and procedures for emergencies are only one aspect. Developing relationships with partner organizations and accessing political leaders have been important to improving care and laws protecting the interests and care of persons with mental illness. The two major foci of the chapter's advocacy are addressing quality issues in mental health services and addressing the criminalization of individuals with mental illness. To begin, NULA offers literature such as a pamphlet for the Los Angeles County's Mental Health Court Linkage program, which provides advocacy and continuity of care when someone is arrested.[44] The group's local involvement was broadened when the women recognized the overincarceration of persons with mental illness. They realized that police and law enforcement officials were often uninformed or unprepared to deal with and recognize the needs and distinctions of a mentally ill African American who is under arrest.

Nancy Carter offered two local stories, the first in which a young African American woman with mental illness was released in the middle of the night after being arrested for a minor crime (failure to pay for her meal at a local restaurant); the young woman disappeared and was never found. In the second incident, a friend's adult son was released from a prison term in which he did not receive medical or psychological services for his mental illness. The man was released without a contact or discharge arrangements and was able to self-medicate with street drugs before calling his family. When the mother finally determined his location, her son, high on drugs, stepped into oncoming traffic and was killed while the mother was on the way to pick him up.[45] These kinds of occurrences inspired "The Color of Justice" program. Goodloe expresses frustration over the issue:

[There is] really poor continuity of care when, unfortunately, mentally ill people get arrested a lot, especially here in LA and I am sure too, in other major cities. Certain ethnicities tend to end up in jails rather than hospitals; where[as] other ethnicities go directly to Cedar Sinai hospital if you catch my drift there. So when people do get arrested, unfortunately, they can be released at any hour of the day or night, which is obviously not conducive for somebody who has mental illness and may not be . . . their judgment or insight may not be so good. It makes no sense whatsoever to release people without a contact or a family member to pick them up.[46]

Carter and Goodloe visit jails and courthouses to provide work-shops, and also anticipate a policy paper and continued lobbying as a part of "The Color of Justice" program. They also sponsored a symposium on the issue through the affiliate chapter.[47] Likewise, the programs for health care professionals served a similar pur-pose after repeated experiences in which insufficient and inaccu-rate care and information were provided or there was inattention to signs of mental illness. As a medical professional, Dr. Goodloe has taken a central role in this area:

> I personally like to talk to other physicians and primary care people
> because again, it's surprising how professionals and health care people
> even have misconceptions about mental illness and don't know all
> the facts and what to do, so that's where I liked it. And we just had
> training, of teaching primary care doctors to sort of quickly recogniz-
> ing mental illness problems . . . a one-page sheet that you could get
> patients to fill out and that can help you tune in to where they are and
> where they need to be helped out on the primary care level or if they
> need to be referred to a psychiatrist, psychologist, specialist. So we
> keep going.[48]

The broadened range of services offered by NULA reflects the *frame extension* stage of the framing process. The group's primary concern for parental support and basic information would even-tually widen to include the broad interests of the actual mental health consumers themselves, veterans of the armed forces, and also training opportunities for law enforcement and medical professionals. With each stage of the process, participants find deeper meaning and reason to sustain their involvement in the social cause while also drawing in more participation and support for their issue, in this case equal access to mental health support and information. Advocacy work is also reflected in their partner-ship with treatment facilities, support programs, and grassroots community research collectives serving Los Angeles County.

Campbell's work as an advocate entailed traveling as a national spokesperson, illuminating the key issues in African American mental health in her fictional work, and using her celebrity to raise awareness about mental illness. The height of Campbell's mental health activism came with the 2005 publication of her fifth and final novel, *72 Hour Hold*, a national best seller that details one mother's battle with an adult daughter who suffers from bipolar disorder. Published just a year before her untimely death, *72 Hour Hold* was produced alongside Campbell's growing advocacy for mental health awareness (chapter 4 provides a close reading of *72 Hour Hold* as an extension of Campbell's activism). The novel would be endorsed as recommended reading for NAMI constituents and families and became central to Campbell's keynote speeches to other parents, medical providers, and policy makers. Campbell's and Carter's advocacy work and involvement in national NAMI efforts established a consistent formal presence impacting the affiliate, African American communities, and NAMI families in general. As the largest African American affiliate in the NAMI network, their advocacy would ultimately result in outreach, support activities, and events on the local and national scale.

In the United States, NAMI is a key mental health advocacy organization. Founded in 1979, NAMI is specifically concerned with severe mental illnesses and provides support for families and lobbies for government programs and policies. In a movement that spans almost four decades, the group has continually and successfully challenged and pressured government organizations and behavioral health efforts to increase research and broaden the definition and outreach of mental illness policies.[49] As the dialogue between independent and federal organizations continues, the fact remains that the concern for individuals and families living with mental illness has become increasingly urgent and that the advocacy movement in the US is active and flourishing.[50]

Some of the long-standing stigma about mental illness includes individuals being considered as unable to make their own health care decisions and also being considered a threat or danger to others. The resulting problems range from poor quality medical treatment, involuntary detention, and other human rights violations. The issues worsen in nations that lack "strong advocacy movements."[51] Ultimately, this movement urges the advancement in quality care and increased awareness about persons living with mental illness. The activism of NAMI, the research from the National Institute on Mental Illness, and the recent emergence of various organizations for research, clinical treatment, advocacy, and community organizing for mental health reform suggest promising shifts within the United States. But until recently, African Americans and nonwhite groups have been underrepresented in these efforts. In the last ten years there has been a growing shift for these communities. Bebe Moore Campbell's national and local work with NAMI and her local affiliate, NULA, has been integral in breaking the silence and increasing mental health awareness, support, and resources for communities of color.

The women leading NULA eventually extended their reach beyond the local scene and became involved in creating change at the systemic level by aligning with the national NAMI network in the fight for policy and institutional changes for people with mental illness. The affiliate website maintains updates on the national dialogue on mental illness, the impact of health care reform, and new research and studies on mental illness and treatment. For instance, Nancy Carter issued a statement on homelessness and mental illness on behalf of the national organization, which was addressed to the US House of Representatives.[52] At the same time, Campbell became an official spokesperson for NAMI and worked actively to increase awareness and resources for families. She traveled and shared the experiences of the circle of African American mothers who started NULA. She also sought to challenge the shame and stigma of mental illness experienced in black communities and encouraged NAMI to initiate formal steps and programs to address the distinct mental health needs of African Americans.

Another major effort that centralized all of the affiliates is the birth of National Minority Mental Health Month in July.[53] Nancy Carter calls this the "coming out" time for those living with the secret shame about mental illness. After Campbell's death and joint efforts and lobbying from supporters and partner organizations, the month was renamed as Bebe Moore Campbell National

Minority Mental Health Month. Dr. Goodloe points to this time as a great opportunity to "recognize mental health issues, challenges, solutions, and improvement."[54] During the month of July, a national effort is launched with events, information, and outreach in order to increase awareness, to address mental health care issues and disparities, and to erase the long-held stigmas associated with mental illness.

Similarly, NAMI's national office launched the Multicultural Action Center. The Multicultural Action Center features resources for African American, Latino, Native American, Asian, and Pacific Islander communities, and provides cultural competency training support for state and government health agencies. Its website offers resources and special programs, like the "In Living Color" educational course for medical professionals, which is also included in the service roster for the NULA affiliate. It also provides a toolkit called "Sharing Hope," designed specifically for outreach in African American church congregations. Although social stigmas and religiosity have often inhibited and discouraged acknowledgment and help-seeking among African Americans with mental health concerns, some argue for creating support networks that build upon the distinct nature of the Black Church, its influence, and its structure.[55]

Black churches can provide African American members with "fellowship, friendships, and moral support . . . [and] this sense of belonging provides a therapeutic group function in that it motivates and facilitates its members to feel, act, and think in ways that are proactive, constructive, and positive."[56]

NAMI's Multicultural Action Network, which is directly influenced by Campbell and her NULA cohorts, is a rich example of meaningful outreach for African Americans. The "Sharing Hope" initiative thus reaches across the stigmas and problems, and draws upon the inherent value in the Black Church's therapeutic tools such as pastoral prayer, grief work, music, and faith healing. Since Campbell's death, the Multicultural Action Network has had a primary role in NAMI's observance of Bebe Moore Campbell National Minority Health Month and offers activities, projects, and initiatives that have been sponsored in communities of color each July throughout the United States.

The NULA affiliate's focus on advocacy builds upon the other areas of education and support and conveys the final stage of the framing process, *frame transformation*. In an effort to cope with the challenges of their children with mental illness, Campbell and the founding women of the affiliate moved from mutual support, to resource gathering, then to full-fledged community outreach. At the advocacy stage, however, their vision transformed in many ways to include ideas that were not a part of their original mission or concern. Starting with the outreach for veterans, then lobbying for national policy change, the group ultimately began to rethink and reshape how mental health is viewed in African American communities. Their focus shifted to challenging and erasing the long-held stigmas and myths within African American cultural history. Along with challenging the fear of being seen as "crazy" and collective anxieties about mistreatment from law enforcement and medical professionals, Campbell's work within the national organization began to address the emotional and spiritual needs of African Americans. By initiating multicultural outreach efforts, this activism transcended the perception that spiritual practice and counseling services are conflicting. Furthermore, it created programs to partner with black churches to promote mental health awareness and support to communities. This, along with the annual National Minority Mental Health Month each July, represents a growing shift and transformation about the normalcy and acceptance of mental illness and the importance of resources, policy change, and open dialogue about mental health. In this final shift, the mothers made quite a jump from the important work of mutual support and prayer to ultimately become a part of a national movement that is shifting the dialogue and consciousness about mental health.

The affiliate members, staff, consumers, family, and friends are involved in other engaging community activities and outreach efforts. One that stands out is the therapeutic use of art by NULA and its support groups. The affiliate enlisted Beverly Heath as a local artist-in-residence. Heath offers an annual workshop series in which family and consumer participants create works of art from found objects in their environment. In the past this has culminated with a celebration and an art showcase of the final creations. This sort of project provides participants with a creative, expressive outlet as they cope. The use of art and creative work, something that Campbell valued, was also a part of the affiliate's opening festivities, which included a staged reading of Campbell's unpublished play, *Even with the Madness*. Actress and NULA cofounder Judyann Elder collaborated with Campbell to workshop the play and bring it to audiences for this important event.[57] These activities, workshops, info fairs, and festival events invite African Americans to open up and seek help for managing mental illness in themselves and in loved ones. Participation in the NAMI Walks for Minds of America event is an important and fun annual event for the affiliate. Held each fall during the first weekend in October, the event provides fund-raising opportunities while increasing visibility for mental health and wellness. In 2007 the NULA office participated with a team of walkers called "Bebe's Victory Squad" in honor of their beloved friend and community member.

On a personal level, Campbell's quest for information and involvement in NAMI extended in many directions. As the group of women took steps toward a formal structure, Campbell was able to utilize her position as a public figure in the interest of mental health awareness. Campbell became actively involved with the national efforts of NAMI, attending conferences and conventions across the United States and regional meetings in the state of California. In addition to becoming a family educator, Campbell also began speaking to audiences of families, medical professionals, and policy makers. With her celebrity and reputation as a best-selling author and journalist, her name and face would also be a resource for the local affiliate as well. Following the work of the NULA founders, there would be an increase in programs, initiatives, and literature that catered to people of color in the national organization. Following her death in 2006, NAMI's national executive director issued a statement recounting her contribution to the organization's cause:

> Bebe was trained as a teacher in NAMI's Family-to-Family education program, as a member of our NAMI Urban Los Angeles affiliate. She attended NAMI conventions and conferences. She was a national spokesperson for us, speaking out against the stigma that often surrounds mental illness, and promoting treatment and family education. Because of her commitment, NAMI's name and voice was heard in countless newspaper, radio and television interviews, touching millions of Americans. Bebe spoke from experience. She spoke from the heart. She spoke for NAMI. We are grateful for all that she shared.[58]

This is essentially why Campbell is an important figure and activist of the contemporary period. Her collective contributions and direct service to communities and families are an important model of committed work for social change.

Within the local affiliate, Lynn Goodloe enjoyed and often took the lead with educational efforts, and Nancy Carter made great strides in the area of advocacy. Campbell and Carter would become key players and primary advocates for promoting diversity within NAMI, and they ushered in the push to increase outreach and support for nonwhite consumers and families. While Campbell was active in all areas within the affiliate, she was particularly inclined to focus on the support efforts. Drawn to creative expression, she participated in nontraditional tactics consistent with bridge leadership, such as art-making in support group meetings for mental health consumers. She would also lend her own creativity toward this cause when she began to fuse her writing career with her activist work. Her heart-wrenching and final novel *72 Hour Hold* would be added to the recommended reading list for NAMI members. Likewise for families with young children, Campbell's earlier book, *Sometimes My Mommy Gets Angry*, offered a compassionate fictional narrative that provided specific strategies for youngsters who have a mentally ill parent. The children's book also received NAMI's 2003 Outstanding Media Award. Campbell remained active in NAMI's national activities as a keynote speaker and spokesperson through her late stages of cancer.

This period in Campbell's life, from her daughter's diagnosis in 1998 to the writer's death in 2006, was a time of immense change. Preceding her journey with family mental illness and intense advocacy, she had established a solid career as an award-winning author and had nurtured strong marital and familial relationships. Her participation in premarital counseling and a couple's support group foreshadowed her orientation toward preventative care and maintenance of social relationships and personal mental health. Campbell has been described as one who was fully engaged in her craft, her community, and the love for her friends and family. Yet the battle with mental illness would rock all that she envisioned and hoped for her family. Nonetheless, the mothers' prayer group and the nonprofit organization that she would later cofound brought about an open path to healing and health for Campbell and countless others. The overall impact of Campbell's activism and that of her cofounders cannot be fully measured at present. Their work yielded a flurry of national and local gains for NAMI and the NULA affiliate. The increased attention to African American mental health is considerable, and yet the work continues. At present there is significant growth in programs, resources, and support that did not exist ten years ago, but disparities for nonwhite consumers of mental health services persist. NAMI's Multicultural Action Center cites the Surgeon General's warning about these inequities, which reports that minorities are less likely to receive diagnosis and treatment for mental illness; have less access to mental health services; often receive poorer quality health care; and are underrepresented in mental health research.[59]

Presently, NULA continues its efforts for this cause. Although Campbell did not live to enjoy the establishment of a community office for the affiliate, in 2005 the group made the shift to a permanent space for its headquarters in the Leimert Park neighborhood of South Los Angeles.[60] This urban community location offered greater access to African American constituents across class groups in an area with a strong history of cultural pride and self-sufficiency.[61] NULA continues its fund-raising efforts with an annual gala event in memory of Campbell, and also participates in the NAMI walks each October.[62] Ellis Gordon succeeded his wife as the treasurer of the affiliate, and Nancy Carter remains active in the political efforts of the national parent organization. There are also new partnerships, including a promising relationship with youth education organizations that seek to mobilize high school and college students in the campaign for mental health awareness.[63]

Much like her years at the University of Pittsburgh decades earlier, we find that Campbell's activism was situated in a collective leadership style. While she possessed far more prominence and agency with NULA than in the Black Action Society, she is still inclined to a collaborative work model. Yet while the mothers embraced a shared leadership model, each woman would find her own niche in serving the NULA affiliate chapter. For Nancy Carter, it was teaching classes and leading daily operations as executive director, and for Lynn Goodloe, it was serving as president of the board of directors and coteaching workshops and informational sessions, particularly those at local churches and for medical professionals. Robnett's discussion of women bridge leaders applies to Campbell and her colleagues' activism within NAMI and NULA. As a formal community bridge leader, Campbell's grassroots work, combined with her fame as an acclaimed author, yielded influence at the local, state, and national levels.[64] In her position as treasurer, she used her innovation and celebrity to gather resources necessary for NULA's cause. However, she also operated in a free space not typical of formal leaders, and was present for court dates and home and jail emergencies when families in the NULA network needed help. This ground-level work was also evident in her role as a support group leader. In this intimate talk space, Campbell utilizes the personal and emotional interaction as a path to transformation. Thus she connects NULA's constituency to its commitment to mental health awareness and support for African Americans.[65] She would continue to exhibit the initiative and passion that were consistent in her life and her work. She was excellent at generating ideas and inspiring and mobilizing people to act. And, of course, there was her writing.

Campbell's writing about mental illness was often the major focus of her speaking engagements and tours and, with her fifth and final novel, would be the definitive marriage between her writing career and her activism. Through her creative fiction, Campbell would effectively burst open "the closet" of fear and shame around mental illness. This extension of her grassroots activism with NULA would also leave a far-reaching and considerable legacy of her commitment to this cause.

Part II moves from the narrative of Campbell's direct activism and, through close reading of her novels, connects her social movement work to her novels. Frame theory is used to explore how her first and final novels bridge, amplify, and extend the sociopolitical work of the BAS and NULA. Together chapters 3 and 4 reveal Campbell's intention and ability to use fiction to transform ideas for her readers and encourage a critical consciousness of social issues in the United States using a signature style that emerges in her fiction.

# Part Two

---

Reading Campbell's First and
Last Novels as Activist Text

# A Novel Beginning: Campbell's Emergence as a Fiction Writer with *Your Blues Ain't Like Mine*

*To me, there's no point in writing merely to entertain. I have*
*to entertain, because if I don't entertain you, you're not*
*going to continue reading. But if I'm not out to enlighten, or*
*change your mind about something, or change your behavior,*
*then I really don't want to take the journey.*
—Bebe Moore Campbell, interview by *Time*, August 6, 2005

For those who knew Bebe Moore Campbell well or just briefly, it was clear that the years at the University of Pittsburgh were pivotal for her, particularly as evidenced by her ongoing commitment and involvement as an alumna.[1] As a young collegian, her writing and worldview were uniquely influenced by the social unrest and change occurring nationally and locally during her childhood and college years in the 1950s and 1960s. The development of her consciousness as rooted in this early activism of her youth held direct implications for her future writing. Her first work of fiction, *Your Blues Ain't Like Mine*, proved to be a groundbreaking entry into the literary world for the novelist and would highlight themes that most certainly resonate with the black student activism at Pitt and throughout the nation in the era of black liberation.

Following her graduation from the University of Pittsburgh in 1971, Campbell's career path would eventually lead to a full-time vocation as a bona fide writer and journalist,[2] thus fulfilling her call and her interests as an undergraduate at Pitt.[3] During the early 1980s she took an interest in fiction writing. She honed her craft in writing workshops, composed short stories, and faced a shower of rejections typical of many early career writers. She began her writing career freelancing, and her work was published in the *New York Times*, the *Washington Post*, the *Los Angeles Times*, *USA Today Weekend*, *Black Enterprise*, and *Ebony*.

In 1986, after beginning her work as a journalist, Campbell published her first nonfiction work, *Successful Women, Angry Men: Backlash in the Two-Career Marriage*. This book was the offshoot of a well-received magazine feature on shifting gender roles and marriage. In 1990 she released her second book, *Sweet Summer: Growing Up with and without My Dad*, a memoir of her upbringing and a commentary on black male parenting. Campbell worked diligently through the rocky beginnings of her writing career, experimenting with magazine articles, short stories, and nonfiction before she eventually found her niche as a novelist.

Although Campbell was a quite formidable journalist, she is best known for her award-winning fiction. The year 1992 brought the release of her debut novel, *Your Blues Ain't Like Mine*.[4] While this was over two decades after her years at Pitt, her first work of fiction resonates with key themes and content that align with the racial consciousness of the 1960s black liberation movement. Her debut was a best seller, and she began receiving increased media attention and critical acclaim after the release of *Your Blues*. This pivotal work won her the NAACP Image Award and a large and diverse readership throughout the United States. Similarly, *all* of her subsequent novels became best sellers on the *New York Times* and *Los Angeles Times* lists as well.

Campbell penned five novels prior to her death, and in each she employed her signature style—a winning formula that boosted her appeal to a wide audience of readers. As she honed her craft, her writing remained creative and authentic, with each work capturing new themes and literary devices. All of Campbell's publications—five novels, two nonfiction books, three children's books—have been dedicated to examining the socioeconomic, political, and personal experiences and dilemmas of African American people. Her fiction has maintained a steady commercial following (though African American women were the initial stronghold of Campbell's readership). The richness of her writing and the import of her content expanded her audience broadly, and she became popular among men and women of various ages, ethnicities, and social classes. Despite her wide popularity and mainstream readership (or because of it), her work is rarely considered in academic discourse. Very often there is a divide constructed between popular fiction and "literary" fiction, which can result in the devaluation and dismissal of significant black women intellectuals and writers. Campbell is one such writer and thinker who cannot be left in the margins. Her work offers the possibility of examining multiple discourses and themes. Additionally, her fiction and nonfiction writing possess compelling value and instructive potential for all, especially African American readers. Campbell's novels have highlighted relevant topics such as mental health, racism in the workplace, interracial friendships and relationships, African American music and entertainment, racialized violence, and police brutality.

To analyze Campbell's fiction, I utilize frame theory,[5] which is essentially a process of building the momentum around a social cause or movement. As described by Snow et al., frame theory includes these four frame alignment processes: *frame bridging*—providing information to those most likely to be interested in a social cause; *frame amplification*—elaborating on the values and beliefs associated with a cause to clarify how it aligns with the individual's personal concerns, thus convincing them that their participation is crucial; *frame extension*—broadening the focus to incorporate concerns not originally a part of the cause; *frame transformation*—the point when frames or value positions are shifted substantially, helping individuals to challenge their deeply held beliefs.[6] Similar to Campbell's bridge leadership, the strength of Campbell's writing is the way she enacts frame theory to connect readers to an idea or ideas that are sociopolitical in nature. Campbell advances her written ideas similar to the way that activists and bridge leaders advance social causes. As a writer-activist, Campbell's activism and fiction work together to further the social justice issues facing African American communities.

In *Your Blues Ain't Like Mine* we are introduced to Bebe Moore Campbell's intellectual and political voice with stark clarity and maturity—an undeniable product of her college years. As a novelist, she uses her characters to express her standpoint on history, race, gender, and society. She tells us what is most important to her, most urgent in her thinking, and what she wants readers to receive from her writing. With her first novel, Campbell offers an intimate look at racialized violence in America's rural South during the era of segregation. Because she writes for a broad popular audience—and engages the complex interplay of history, race, gender, sex, and violence—her impact is profound and noteworthy. Set in Hopewell, Mississippi, and Chicago and spanning four decades (late 1950s to the late 1980s), *Your Blues* offers a fictitious rendering of the lynching, trial, and aftermath of the infamous Emmett Till murder case. In *Your Blues* Campbell examines the long-term impact of racism and the tensions of black and white communities living and working in close proximity. Published twenty-two years after the birth of the Black Action Society (BAS), Campbell's first novel articulates a crisp racial consciousness and sociopolitical commentary. Through textual analysis, this chapter examines Campbell's focus and commentary on African American historical memory; black women's racialized gender experience; white racism, class, and patriarchy; and forgiveness, healing, and redemption in the novel. Across these themes it is evident that the personal and political ideas that Campbell developed as a collegian during the black liberation era continued to evolve as she penned her first novel. The overflow of her student activist years clearly undergirds her approach to writing and the focus on social issues and sociopolitical themes.

As the novel commences, the Cox men—patriarchs of a working-poor white family—brutally murder fifteen-year-old Armstrong Todd. They accuse the northern black boy of speaking inappropriately to a white woman, Lily Cox, in her husband's pool hall. After national media coverage, the entire country takes notice of the continued segregation and social injustice in Hopewell, Mississippi. The town of Hopewell is turned upside down when this typical crime of white violence and lynching of black citizens yields increased attention and discontent. Although the three Cox men are acquitted for the black boy's murder, the story has just begun. The town of Hopewell is forever changed because of the national attention that the lynching brings. The black citizens feel embittered by the acquittal, but also become bolder and more self-assured. Armstrong's murder has personal impact and even consequence for several individuals and families, black and white. With a nuanced and compassionate depiction of personality, self-awareness, and relationship, Campbell crafts well-developed characters that are male and female, black and white, rich and poor.

Campbell writes the lives of twenty-three regularly occurring characters in *Your Blues Ain't Like Mine*. Through close reading, I examine these primary and secondary characters as vehicles for each of the four recurring themes within the novel. I argue that the characterization in *Your Blues* is the mechanism by which Campbell establishes and voices her ideological standpoint as a writer-activist. With this textual analysis, I demonstrate how she utilizes her characters for this purpose, according to the four signature themes I have identified in *Your Blues*.

In her own words, Campbell wrote *Your Blues* with the intention of rethinking historical fiction:

> I did not want this to be an historical novel. I didn't want to stay true to the story. I was more interested in creating something similar and then really exploring my premise that racism is a crime for which we all pay—not just the victims, but the perpetrators as well. Carrying this out to the next generation, how this murder continues to vibrate in these lives—that's what I wanted to do.[7]

Campbell's awareness of and investment in African American historical memory reflect her black nationalist leanings and academic experience in black studies while at the University of Pittsburgh. Using a variety of literary mechanisms, she establishes a sense of historicity within each of her five novels. Whether writing a fictional account of a historical event, connecting past and present stories with flashbacks, or utilizing epic memory as a tool, Campbell always integrates African American historical legacy in each of her novels. In *Your Blues Ain't Like Mine* Campbell initiates her signature style and creatively employs the use of historical memory in contemporary fiction. She begins *Your Blues* as a traditional historical narrative set in the 1950s rural South and, by the end of the novel, travels forward to a contemporary setting circa 1989. Published in 1992, *Your Blues* can be read as both contemporary and historical fiction at once because, rather than remaining in a single period of time, the novel spans four decades in African American life and history.

The novel's plot is initiated with the lynching of a young black boy, Armstrong Todd, who is visiting his grandmother in Hopewell, Mississippi, for the summer. This pivotal event in the narrative is a direct reference to the real-life lynching of Emmett Till in 1955 in Money, Mississippi. Both in Campbell's fictional account and in the Till murder, national outrage and mourning gave way to an upsurge of civil rights activism in response to the slaughter of innocent black children.[8] Campbell deliberately uses this historical moment not only as an act of remembrance but also as a site for examining the complexities of black life in the face of white racism. She utilizes this historical moment as reflection and reference for later social ills and perils faced by black male youth in urban inner-city settings in the 1980s, thus creating a social discourse that mirrors her black nationalism politics as a student activist at Pitt. With this connection Campbell enacts several stages of the framing process, first by *bridging* her readers to the social issue of racial violence in general. For those familiar with racial violence in a historical context, she *amplifies* their concern by connecting lynching to contemporary urban violence, posing the two as connected and equally important. For readers who chose the novel for primary literary interests, she *extends* their interest in engaging fictional narrative by including sociopolitical discourse. This literary framing is also closely tied to her editorial work for the BAS newspaper at the University of Pitt, where she wrote about police violence against college student activists during the period. Racial violence becomes one site of intellectual discourse that Campbell deems important and thus introduces it to her readers. She engages in this frame shifting with the intention of challenging and expanding the conceptual location of her audience.

Campbell is clearly concerned about racial violence and socio-economic inequities that undergird such violence at the time she writes *Your Blues Ain't Like Mine*. Armstrong's murder revisits the painful legacy of lynching and racial violence tracing back, before the plantations of US enslavement, to the horrific terrorism of the Middle Passage and the transatlantic slave trade. This same racial violence extends forward in the form of police brutality, a primary concern among 1960s Black Power and black student activists. Campbell and her colleagues protested local and national incidences of police brutality in African American communities and against black students on college campuses across the United States. Accordingly, the concerns of that period influenced Campbell's understanding of and concern for the historical context of such violence. Her focus on racial violence elucidates the historical and institutional devaluation of black life in all periods of American and world history, such that the recurring incidents of violence against African and black people is normalized and often goes unpunished. The brutal lynching of Armstrong Todd in *Your Blues* exposes just one moment in time when racial violence and terrorism seemingly go unchecked until the local community decides to respond and resist. The situation of Armstrong's death helps contextualize the racial violence inherited from enslavement that precedes this time period, and the increasing visibility of police brutality and intraracial violence of the period to follow. Resistance to this legacy of violence would spur the modern civil rights movement in the United States, with young people at its forefront.[9] Also, within the subtext of the novel, the sexual and gendered complexities of racial hostility and violence arise. Armstrong Todd, like Emmett Till, is murdered because he is accused of speaking inappropriately to a white woman (also later in the novel, and true to historical trend, Campbell depicts the attempted rape of a black woman by a white male authority figure). Ultimately, through Armstrong's character, Campbell exposes America's legacy of lynching and racialized violence as an impetus that spurred the era of civil rights.

Campbell enacts *frame extension* (broadening the focus to incorporate new concerns) by connecting racial violence to socio-economic inequities in the United States, both in the rural South and the industrialized North. While one can glean that racial violence has been a pervasive issue in African American life and history, much of *Your Blues* is situated in the rural southern town of Hopewell, Mississippi, and thus the novel illustrates the shifting economic and social structure of the Delta region. This includes the accompanying trend of black migration, which denotes the mass movement of blacks to northern cities to escape the terror, poverty, and hopelessness of the Jim Crow South. Those who remained would continue to suffer the exploitative practice of sharecropping[10] and its "evolution" toward equally oppressive industrial models of labor and employment. In Campbell's fictitious town of Hopewell, there is gradual change with desegregated public facilities and work sites while residential segregation is sustained. In the character Ida Long, we are able to examine these multiple issues and historical moments. Ida lives in the poor area relegated for black sharecroppers, known as the Quarters. She is a friend of Armstrong's family and a big sister figure to the teenage boy. Although the young, spirited woman desires to join the wave of her generation that chose to migrate to northern cities in search of new opportunities, unfortunate circumstances require Ida to remain in Hopewell to care for her family. Though Ida never leaves Hopewell, the single mother becomes proactive in cultivating change in the small rural town, for the sake of her son, Sweetbabe, and the other citizens in her community.

Early in the novel, in the years following Armstrong's murder, Ida works as a maid by day and sells dinners on the side. She begins to host "rent" parties to raise money for her dream of moving to Chicago. Modeled after activists in the Student Nonviolent Coordinating Committee (SNCC), two northern black men, working as voter registration activists, canvass the area and find their way to Ida's weekend party looking for food, drinks, and new recruits. One of the young men, Dan, has an intense but fleeting courtship with Ida. As he and his colleague seek volunteers to register to vote, Ida is both fearful and inspired. Ultimately, a local black church is bombed after four black men from Hopewell attempt to register to vote. While the northerners are eventually run out of town, this plotline eventually leads to the increased politicization of the residents, who gradually begin to speak up for themselves and to organize and respond to the racial terror and economic and social inequities in Hopewell. While the national emphasis on civil rights activism increased during the period, in reality these efforts often seemed peripheral to the daily lives of Campbell's black characters. However, the black citizens of Hopewell, energized by the national struggle for civil rights, would eventually become more active and vocal about discrimination and inequity in the small Mississippi town.

A key shift in the social and economic structure of the South was the shift from agriculture to industrialization. Stirred by the arrival of voter registration activists, the black townsfolk in Hopewell gradually evolve from helpless outrage over Armstrong's murder to courage, activating a permanent sense of agency to improve the living and working conditions in their small rural community. Hopewell is a fictional Mississippi Delta town of poor black sharecroppers, wealthy white landowners, and a poor white working class. However, Campbell depicts life in Mississippi with vivid and accurate historical detail. In actuality, the Delta's primarily agrarian economy begins to shift by the 1960s when a postwar decline sets in and cotton farming is increasingly co-opted by large businesses and corporations. Within the fictional narrative of *Your Blues*, the New Plantation Catfish Farm and Processing Plant serves as a symbol of the shifting economic structure as local landowners attempt to reorganize and sustain their business holdings in the area. As the town's fiscal and civic leaders orchestrate the development of the New Plantation Catfish Farm and Processing Plant, the black citizens and poor whites become totally reliant on the company for steady work and income—just as they did in a sharecropping system. The appropriately named New Plantation does not improve work conditions or quality of life for the former sharecroppers who come to work in the factory.

Ida, along with other locals, is hired at New Plantation and is subject to grueling and demeaning work conditions no better than the fieldwork of the old plantation. After several years she begins to organize black and white workers to protest the inhumane conditions at the plant and demand better treatment of workers. This plotline demonstrates the shifts and changes that, rather than denoting progress, usher in a different kind of oppression and exploitation of the labor force. From the plantation to the factory, poor workers found themselves in the same rut—neither able to earn an income beyond subsistence nor able to avoid the toll and wear on their bodies from grueling physical labor. This narrative is grounded in historical trends in labor and the southern economy.[11] Campbell effectively depicts the intricate web of segregation, lynching/violence, migration, labor/employment, economic subsistence, and industrialization in the North and South alike. This sort of integrated analysis mirrors black studies scholarship and is consistent with Campbell's education and politicization as a student at Pitt. However, within contemporary fiction in the early 1990s, *Your Blues* advances a unique political depth and historical analysis compared to other works within the same genre.

Alternatively, in the Chicago setting of *Your Blues*, the Todd family illustrates the impact and intersection of southern history and racism with northern migration and continued hardship as the nation's economic and racial politics collide in the contemporary period. Estranged husband and wife, Delotha and Wydell Todd, are parents of the slain youth, Armstrong Todd. As migrants from the South they initially sought a better life in the Windy City, free of poverty and racial terror. Delotha takes personal responsibility for having sent her son to the South and also laments the absence of her alcoholic husband, Wydell. Wydell Todd is a man who is disillusioned with life in the North. For many blacks, migrating north promised freedom from racial terrorism and sharecropping, but also brought new challenges and perils such as labor-intensive factory work, unfair wages and work conditions, and the urban lure of alcohol and drug use. The couple reunites, shortly after Armstrong's death, when Wydell sobers up, recommits himself to his wife, and prepares for a career as a barber. Through these characters, *Your Blues* connects the struggle for civil rights and issues of racialized violence and inequality in the rural South (in the 1950s and 1960s) with the urban issues of the North and continued social and economic inequality that African Americans faced (in the 1970s and 1980s). For many blacks who migrated north, industrialized cities like Chicago posed new forms of racial disparity and economic hardship. Campbell writes the post–civil rights era effectively by depicting issues such as housing discrimination, unemployment, and low-wage employment for uneducated southern transplants. She then utilizes the Todd family to highlight the historical shifts of the 1970s and 1980s, examining the impact of crack cocaine and the Reagan administration on black communities. For Delotha and Wydell, the unhealed trauma of Armstrong's lynching takes its toll and affects how they raise their youngest son, WT.

Wydell and Delotha also carry the baggage of growing up in segregated Mississippi, and believe that they must protect their son from "white folks" who wish to do harm to young black males. They are shortsighted about the complex problems and imminent dangers of urban America in the 1980s. They fail to understand that there are more immediate threats to WT than the overt white racism and violence that plagued their own childhoods in the 1940s South. In one scene Delotha talks to a client about local Chicago politics and the death of their first and only African American mayor, Harold Washington (this lets us know that the year is now 1987). Delotha states, "Most of them white boys on the city council didn't want nobody black in there in the first place." Maudine shifts the racial commentary and tells Delotha, "If we could just keep these children off these drugs. . . . That's the problem."[12] Campbell uses this moment to introduce commentary on the problems African Americans faced during the Reagan era, such as "black-on-black" crime, drug use and trafficking of crack cocaine, and other residual outcomes of the "War on Drugs" policies that plagued urban neighborhoods (increased incarceration and harsher sentencing for poor black offenders). The two women grapple to engage and make sense of the social ills and issues facing black people. Delotha becomes anxious and thinks of her teenage son, WT, and his growing attraction to the street life.

Campbell concludes Delotha's inner dialogue with the thought that "all her life she'd been defending him against the wrong enemy; she would have to fight the streets to save him, and she didn't have the strength."[13] Here we see Delotha, as a late-age parent in her sixties, challenged by how to raise and protect her son from contemporary social dangers. We also see the misperception that black people, particularly black males, have a single enemy or threat. Historically, white racism was most obvious in overt forms of violence, prejudice, and discrimination, rather than in the complex institutional manifestations of poverty, crime, drugs, unemployment, and homelessness. Realizing this, Delotha comes full circle when her unhealed wounds about Armstrong's murder emerge alongside her fear of losing another son, WT, to street life and gang involvement.

As the plot climaxes, police visit Delotha at home inquiring about WT's involvement in a robbery, and she perceives the white police officers in 1980s Chicago with the same distrust and anguish as the white lynchers in 1950s Mississippi. She goes to see Wydell's cousin, Lionel, for help and exclaims, "All I ever wanted was for WT to be safe, for white people not to kill him like they done Armstrong."[14] Lionel proclaims, "The streets is killing more black boys than the white folks ever could. We always had more than one enemy."[15] Here Campbell attempts to articulate the complexity of racism and its institutional manifestations across many facets of African American life. To be specific, circa 1985, the impact of the Reagan administration was felt heavily in poor black and Latino communities. Accordingly, Campbell continues to situate the fictional account into the social realities of black people, which shifts with each decade. The economic policies of the Reagan presidency[16] cut programs that aided poor black communities and resulted in sustained poverty and increased unemployment. During this time the government increased defense spending, provided tax cuts for the very wealthy, and failed to increase the minimum wage in the eight years that Reagan was in office. With an increased budget deficit and national debt, the impact on poor and black communities was felt in myriad ways. The 1980s saw increased drug and alcohol use as an overflow from the 1970s and a rise in violence and criminal activity. Persistent poverty and low quality of life preceded the adjacent phenomena of teen gang involvement and the use and sale of narcotics in urban neighborhoods. Simultaneously, the War on Drugs policy and mandatory minimum sentencing that punished crack possession more heavily than cocaine possession created racial disparities in prosecution and sentencing for drug-related offenses.[17] The impact manifested in neighborhoods and prisons and continued to worsen during the 1980s with a specific effect on young black males. Campbell posits this transition as a sort of neo-lynching, with Armstrong and WT at the center of each period's perils for black boys. Once again, contrasting black life in rural Hopewell in the 1950s and 1960s to black inner-city life in Chicago is Campbell's effort to shift the conceptual frame her readers. She *amplifies* the social ills of the early period and broadens the scope of concern to *extend* to contemporary political issues.

Although this is not stated explicitly in the narrative of *Your Blues*, Campbell hints at the political climate of the time by mentioning presidential elections and major political, economic, and social shifts and incidents to advance the novel's timeline. With skillful depictions of characters and setting, Campbell narrates a timeline of nearly four decades in African American experience. Readers of contemporary popular fiction receive a poignant story of families, neighbors, and communities. Campbell situates these narratives in the remembrance of southern lynching, sharecropping, segregation, and the civil rights struggle. *Your Blues* nods at the changing tides of desegregation, voting rights, and the exodus of African Americans out of the rural South into northern cities. Through the latter segment of the Chicago plotline, Campbell exposes new problems of internalized and systemic issues that would serve to undermine the social and physical well-being of black communities and individuals through a more subtle and institutionalized racism and the growing War on Drugs.

By actively using the memory device as a bridge, Campbell demonstrates her value for historical experience as a context for present-day problems and the continuity of the struggle against racial, social, and economic injustice experienced by African American people. This directly reflects on the prominent concerns and issues of race, masculinity, and politics of the 1960s black liberation era. Thus the priorities and values of Campbell's college years clearly resonate in her first novel, *Your Blues Ain't Like Mine*. The reader sees how American history and politics inform her plotline and the lives of her characters. In *Your Blues Ain't Like Mine* Bebe Moore Campbell masterfully uses historical memory as a vehicle and metaphor to advance her viewpoint on a myriad of concerns facing black communities in the context of this country's vexed social and racial history. A clear evolution from the social consciousness that was sparked during the writer's time as a student activist at the University of Pittsburgh, Campbell demonstrates precision and maturity in her understanding of the complexities of US racial history and inequity in the historical fabric weaved together in *Your Blues Ain't Like Mine*. Just as she used writing, political organizing, and personal relationships to mobilize and maintain student activism, she later integrates fiction, sociopolitical analysis, and her complex understanding of humanity to broaden the views of her readers about contemporary issues (and their historical roots).

Campbell's increasing concern with black women's experiences in her college years, as a founding member of Black Women For Black Men, emerges with greater precision in *Your Blues*. She writes for a broad audience and provides well-developed male and female characters; thus it would be erroneous to classify her solely as a women's writer just because she is female. More accurately, Campbell has proven to effectively address the experiences of particular identity groups and ensures that black women's narratives emerge with great detail and authenticity. In *Your Blues Ain't Like Mine* her characters often symbolize black women's sociopolitical positions without reinscribing prevailing stereotypes or archetypes. The female characters Delotha, Ida, Willow, and Marguerite are highlighted here to explore the lives of black women in a US historical context and their experiences within the novel. (The white female character, Lily, is addressed in a subsequent section.)

Having migrated north to Chicago to escape the perils of southern violence and economic oppression, Delotha attempts a new life with better opportunities. Neither she nor her son Armstrong engages in deference to white male power or embrace feelings of black inferiority. Delotha is a black woman making social progress—she establishes some economic power and independence as an entrepreneur and hairstylist. But she copes with other problems, such as the disillusionment of life in the North and struggling to rear her son alone as a working mother. She sends Armstrong south to live with her mother so that she can get on her feet. As a result, Delotha Todd finds herself in the most unenviable position a parent could have, which is to bury her own child. While resting at her mother's home, she recalls Armstrong's wailing departure for Hopewell and his pleas to return to Chicago. Delotha moans aloud, "God is punishing me, Mama. He's punishing me for being a bad mother." When her mother, Odessa, blames her absent husband, Wydell, Delotha's crying stops short. Feeling deep resentment, Delotha remarks: "There ain't no justice for a colored woman, is it, Mama?"[18] She is rightfully distraught and enraged. She channels this raw emotion by exposing her son's lynching and bringing public attention to the viral and murderous racism of Mississippi. She transports Armstrong's body to Chicago for a public funeral and tells her story to journalists. Here Campbell clearly draws from the real-life anguish of Mamie Till-Mobley and the high-profile lynching of Emmett Till. This pivotal moment that fueled the civil rights movement occurred when Campbell was a child herself. Till's murder stuck with Campbell as a child, alongside her direct experience with school desegregation in Philadelphia in the 1960s. Campbell's lived experience and political consciousness precipitate her depiction of these events in her fictional narrative. However, there is also a gendered theme that emerges in Campbell's writing in future works, which is maternal guilt and the trope of the "bad black mother." Delotha's pain and hatred for her son's murderer are commingled with self-criticism and loathing, rooted in the fear that she somehow failed as a single woman and mother.

After talking to a reporter from the *Chicago Courier*, Delotha reads the finished article and recalls her dazed grief: "She didn't recall saying any of the words that the newspaper article said were hers, although the part that read 'I can't forgive, I just can't' sounded familiar."[19] Delotha nurses the unhealed wounds of her loss, and she struggles with her unforgiveness year after year. She never truly forgives herself; her estranged spouse, Wydell; or the men who killed Armstrong. She immerses herself in work and starts a new family with Wydell. She is distant to her own daughters because she fears losing them like she lost Armstrong. Things fall apart when Delotha has another son, Wydell Todd Jr., or WT. Delotha's parental fear shifts from detachment from her daughters to doting and obsessing over her new son. She pushes away her husband and fixates on WT as if he were her long-lost Armstrong reincarnated. She gains weight, neglects her business and family, and fails to realize that she is ill-prepared to parent and rear her son. When the spoiled and undisciplined child becomes a teenager, Delotha is unable to rescue him from the danger he places himself in and his attraction to the local gang scene. She remains in denial but projects her fear and guilt elsewhere and resents Wydell for abandoning her once again. Delotha eventually breaks down and goes to family for help, realizing that she has carried a heavy load for much too long. This marks a turning point for Delotha, foreshadowing the long-awaited acknowledgment of her post-traumatic stress.

Campbell does several things with Delotha's character. Despite her challenges, she is not a fragile victim, nor is she frail in her womanhood. Delotha stands in her right to indignation about her son's murder, and she is unapologetic in her resentment of the white racism and violence that he suffered. She is supportive and seemingly forgiving of Wydell and enterprising enough to envision and cultivate their financial security as proprietors of their own business. She desires a supportive, loving husband rather than a patriarchal provider. Yet Campbell also uses Delotha to illustrate a mother's pain and maternal guilt and the long-term impact of being unable to forgive. Through Delotha we see that the lack of healing over Armstrong's murder is costly and jeopardizes her marriage, her career, and her family. Furthermore, holding on to her anger does little to protect the life of her second son, WT. Suggesting that Delotha should forgive the murderers who took her son's life is a tall order, but Campbell reveals the higher price on Delotha's life and mental health. She challenges mothers who abuse themselves with self-criticism, unforgiveness, and the fear that they have failed as parents. Campbell advances that, like Delotha, women (and men) must reconcile the deep wounds of racism and sexism and process feelings of loss and pain. She creates a moment for Delotha and for her readers to redefine and rethink black motherhood; this is similar to the way she supported and constructed self-defining woman-centered spaces for black female students at Pitt, such as Black Women for Black Men (BWFBM).

Ida Long is introduced as a young single mother living in the segregated section of Hopewell. She is both wise and responsible and saw Armstrong as a younger brother. She is also haunted by the unknown identity of her biological father, a white man whom her mother refused to name before she died. Ida hopes to work hard and escape Hopewell with her son, and move to Chicago, like an entire generation of Mississippi expatriates. But difficult times prevent this, and she spends her savings to help her ailing stepfather and siblings. Ida Long's character challenges stereotypes and offers an unmarried, uneducated woman who has a sound sense of personal agency and a commitment to her son, her family, and her community. Ida has her own demons, including the disappointment of remaining in Hopewell, the unknown identity of her white father, and the pain and guilt she feels about Armstrong's death. When she hears that Armstrong runs into trouble at the pool hall, she hurries to check on him but fails to act or inform his grandmother. She convinces herself that things will be okay, and just hours later she and her stepfather, William, are informed that the boy has been killed. Feeling a sense of guilt and responsibility, Ida matures and is jolted to become a more vocal, proactive person who works actively for the good of those around her. This occurs first in small instances, like insisting on help from a wealthy white man when a rabid dog bites her son and he needs quality medical care. She strives for some economic independence and earns money cooking dinners and hosting Saturday night parties in addition to working as a maid. Ida isn't able to leave for Chicago, but she is able to pay off William's medical bills after an injury, which keeps her family afloat. Later she discovers her interest in community activism, sparked by voter registration activists canvassing in Hopewell. The young organizers from the North help Ida to realize that empowerment is simply a matter of willful action, and this becomes a way of life for her.

Still, Ida is vulnerable to the subjugated position of black women as she suffers harassment from Sheriff Barnes. The older white man begins by extorting bribes from Ida in order to keep her rent parties running. With each collection his visits worsen and his subtle leering becomes more aggressive sexual advances. One evening Ida, who would often run to clear her head, takes a jog through the Quarters. Sheriff Barnes, who has been watching her from the woods, attempts to sexually assault her. Campbell takes this opportunity to illustrate the tenuous position of black women as sexual objects of desire for white men. Sheriff Barnes uses his position of authority to assault Ida and perceives himself as having rightful access to the black woman's body. In her own words, Campbell offers about black women's vulnerability as sexual prey for white men:

> Well, we were raped, of course, with impunity throughout slavery and the post–Emancipation Proclamation Era. Until the Civil Rights Act of 1964, it was always open season on black women. Our honor was not taken seriously, which put black men in a position of always feeling ashamed that they couldn't defend us unless they were willing to pay with their lives. We were the loose and easy targets of racialized sexualization, while white women were put on a pedestal.[20]

Fortunately, this is not Ida's fate, and Sheriff Barnes is painfully put in his place. Later in the novel Ida continues to mobilize and advocate political and social change on behalf of her community. First she cajoles Clayton Pinochet, a wealthy newspaper editor, to tutor her son as he did Armstrong. Later she convinces him to start an instructional program for other black children in the area, while assisting him as a coteacher. As she ages, Ida begins to organize the black and white workers at the New Plantation

Catfish Farm and Processing Plant in the demand for better wages and work conditions. By the end of the novel she is leading a protest to integrate the local senior citizens center and exploring other avenues of fighting discrimination through the legal system. Although remaining in Hopewell was not her intended plan, she plays the cards life has dealt and "blooms" in the rural southern soil in which she has been planted. Ida is able to send her son away, and her alliance with Clayton Pinochet also sets the stage for substantive changes in the town of Hopewell at the institutional level and for her family as well.

Willow Scott, a middle-aged waitress and cook at Hopewell's Busy Bee Café, is unafraid of and even confrontational with whites. Willow is an enigmatic figure in the Hopewell community and is bold, cunning, and agile for a middle-aged woman. She counters many stereotypes about women and blacks in the 1950s rural South. The half-Choctaw woman lives in the woods and is rumored to have slit the throat of a husband who tried to beat her. She is also known to outhunt and outshoot any man. Still, she is also sensitive when Ida comes to ask of her friendship with her late mother and the mysterious identity of Ida's white father. When Ida expresses hatred for the unknown man, Willow offers her this wisdom:

> "Don't do that, child. In life the trick is just to do what's necessary to keep on living. Hating him is like trying to run with a sack of rocks in your drawers. It'll slow you down; might even get you killed. He ain't done right by you, but you remember this here: Life will give you what you deserve, even when people don't. You don't believe that, you just keep on living."[21]

Although she is a minor character, Willow is important because she stands up to white men regularly, thus stepping outside of other black female stereotypes of sex object, victim, mammy, or mistress. This pinnacles when she shoots and injures Sheriff Barnes as he tries to rape Ida and subsequently disappears before she is arrested or tried in court. Willow resurfaces once more in the novel, decades after her disappearance. She appears seemingly out of thin air, when one of Armstrong's murderers, Floyd Cox, is harassing his estranged wife, Lily. Willow, who is dressed like a man and camouflaged in all green, watches Floyd from the woods. He begins to throw rocks at her when he realizes that his observer is a woman. Willow begins to chase him, and he falls to the ground, looks up fearfully, and sees her holding a stone over his head. But rather than doing him any physical harm, she spares him the fate she exacted on Sheriff Barnes. She sees the white man as pitiful and powerless "trash" and walks away chuckling. In both instances Willow supports Lily and Ida in the face of white male terrorism, thus complicating the racial and sexual politics of white male/white female and white male/black female interactions. In her depiction of Willow, Campbell effectively turns the gendered power dynamic on its head. With Willow and the representation of the other black women in the novel, the feminist strivings of her student essay "Black Womanhood Defined" emerge with greater clarity. Campbell consistently reimagines and corrects narrative descriptions of black women and challenges her readers to do the same.

Willow is depicted as irreverent, wise, powerful, mysterious, and brave. Willow comes to Ida's aid, leaving a bullet in Sheriff Barnes, and then retreats back into the woods as mysteriously as she emerged. Campbell's portrayal of Willow rearranges the traditional gender roles prescribed for black females. Willow is a *protector* of women, a role traditionally reserved for men, yet her protection is not accompanied by any subordination. She is able-bodied and athletic, like Ida, and brash, like Delotha, but lives off the land in virtual solitude. She is skilled with a rifle and capable of defending herself (or others) in a physical confrontation. Campbell uses Willow to represent black women's self-reliance and capacity to stand boldly in defense of themselves and their loved ones. She does not advocate violence or instigating conflict, but rather calls for self-sufficiency and confidence—the ability to survive and to be content with one's own company. Willow's independence, intellect, and fearlessness reflect Campbell and her female classmates as she organized with the BAS and served on the Political Action Committee.

Finally, Marguerite, who most obviously resembles the arche-type of a jezebel or concubine, is the ingénue of the softhearted Clayton Pinochet. Marguerite is clear that the relationship is taboo and also realizes that Clayton's love is commingled with white guilt and his desire for solace and comforting. Further-more, the nurturing he seeks from the younger black woman is inextricably tied to his longing for his black caregiver (alternately known as a "mammy"), Etta, the woman responsible for his care and upbringing as a child. Marguerite willingly participates in the sexual and emotional relationship, enjoying the financial comfort and security it provides. The black community shuns her for her relationship with Clayton, and she is perceived by many in the Quarters as prostituting herself to this wealthy white man. Ida Long is one of the few people who is kind to Marguerite, although they are not close friends.

Marguerite eventually grows to desire more for her life. Although the white man believes he truly loves his mistress, Marguerite resists being powerless or possessed by Clayton. She insists that she be taught to read and that the deed to her home is in her own name, and presses him to marry her. Marguerite reflects on all that Clayton has given her but begins to question the relationship as she matures:

> For nearly ten years, all she had ever been concerned about was that Clayton took care of her. He'd rescued her from the winters that whistled through the cracks of her tar-paper shack like a freight train. He'd delivered her from hunger. He'd brought her to a place where she was safe and warm and well fed, but that wasn't enough any longer. She'd never asked him if he thought she was as good as he was, but suddenly that was all she wanted to know.[22]

Although she is labeled by the black community as a "white man's whore," Marguerite's complex romance with the benevolent Clay-ton is more than it seems. While there is certainly genuine affec-tion present, each of them brings a personal agenda impacted by the tense racial relations of the time. Marguerite stands to gain financial security and education that would otherwise be denied her as a black person and a woman. The fact that she has to use sex as a tool of negotiation is historically grounded in the plight of many black/mixed-race women who were deemed attractive by white standards.[23] Her troubled situation bespeaks the vexed confines and limited options of black women of the period. She is a contrast from Ida Long, who, despite her intelligence and beauty, is barely literate, is very poor, and is resigned to stay in Hopewell. Campbell's depiction of Marguerite's character suggests that black woman possess a will to survive despite seemingly humiliating circumstances but also reflects the maturing of a woman's self-worth over time. Marguerite leaves Clayton eventually when his cowardice and inhibition become clear to her. She opts out of the marriage and heads to Chicago, where she completes her high school equivalency degree correspondence course and enrolls in college to become a teacher.

Campbell's portrayal of Clayton's mistress, Marguerite, engages interracial sexual politics with more sophistication and nuance than the days of BWFBM and her undergraduate writing at the University of Pittsburgh. In her college essay "Black Womanhood Defined," we saw Campbell's effort to engage the gender politics of black nationalism. This was an early attempt to use writing as a tool of activism, particularly as a means of *frame extension*—that is, an attempt to accentuate shared values while enlisting support for gender equity and attention to black women's sociopolitical experience.[24] Here in *Your Blues* she does so even more effectively, using the postbellum sexual relationship between Clayton and Marguerite to theorize the complexity of black female positionality throughout history. From the 1960s to the present, black nationalist ideology has struggled with patriarchy and often fallen short of a progressive gender politics. While committed to the broad sociopolitical issues that face African American communities, Campbell's acts of frame shifting within *Your Blues* insist that black women's experiences be included as relevant, important, and equally urgent as the lynching and racial violence experienced by black men and boys.

These four characters, in a novel whose plot centers on race and masculinity, reject the limitations of their gendered and racialized position as black women. Each of them is intelligent, bold, and fearless in her own way. Campbell comments on the interplay of racial and sexual violence, and the vulnerability and objectification of black women by white men, but also restores visibility and personhood through each woman. The women can be vulnerable and brave at once. They are written with authenticity and humanity, and their sensuality and sexuality are not depicted in an objectifying fashion. Ida emerges as a local activist and represents the fruit of hope and determination, while Delotha demonstrates the importance of healing for black women and mothers. Marguerite negotiates her partnership arrangement with a sense of pride and self-worth, rejecting the shame and humiliation her community tries to project onto her. Willow Scott is simply free and unafraid in her freedom. Ultimately, Campbell depicts black women's racialized gender experience with historical accuracy but in a fashion that is liberating rather than tragic or one-dimensional.

Campbell's historicist priorities and commentaries on gender and race are useful, as she seeks to situate the public, private, and economic relationships between black and white characters in her first novel. Once again, her ability to understand white racism reflects the period of her attendance at the University of Pittsburgh on the heels of the King assassination. In *Your Blues* she endeavors an intimate portrayal of a complex southern white citizenry of wealthy elite powerbrokers, would-be liberal allies, and a resentful, impoverished white underclass who cling to their skin-color privilege as their sole stronghold over black residents in the community. Campbell's fictional account skillfully depicts white racial identity formation and complicates stereotypes about white racism. While she excuses neither white privilege nor acts of bigotry, her interpretation offers an understanding of white racial identity that is both exacting and humane. The white characters in *Your Blues* relate to Hopewell's black community according to social class and familial norms. Campbell's careful representation of the personal and structural nature of white racism exposes the intimate face of bigotry and privilege. The novel moves between individual responsibility and the systemic nature of racism, as it interrogates racial issues and ideologies that manifest in the lives of each character. Characters Stonewall Pinochet, Clayton Pinochet, Lily Cox, and Floyd Cox elucidate the unique and varied experiences of Hopewell's poor and wealthy white citizens, as each negotiates privilege, class, power, gender, and violence in relation to the local black community.

Stonewall Pinochet is one of Hopewell's most influential white power brokers. Even though he is neither an elected official nor holds an official position in law enforcement, this wealthy landowner leads the local governing board, the Honorable Men of Hopewell, and virtually runs the entire town and all of its affairs. For example, this governing body covertly imposed higher property taxes for black citizens, while denying their children access to the white schools that their parents subsidized. It denied blacks life insurance, blocked the development of black businesses, and chased the most ambitious blacks out of town toward greater opportunity in the North. Stonewall Pinochet owns a majority of the land in Hopewell, employing and leasing property to most of the black sharecroppers and poor white laborers in the area. Concerned about his legacy and the future of his business interests, the old man hopes his only son, Clayton, will take over his business interests and investments. However, Stonewall regularly derides Clayton for his disinterest in the local white elite class, his career choice as a newspaper editor, his sympathy toward blacks, and most of all his illicit partnership and infatuation with his young black mistress, Marguerite. Stonewall and the Honorable Men of Hopewell shift with the times and decide to turn away from the agrarian economy of the South. In place of a large farming business, they create a lucrative corporate machine with a new local factor, the New Plantation Catfish Farm and Processing Plant. New Plantation would employ and abuse the same poor black and white locals who previously worked as sharecroppers and field hands.

Stonewall and the Honorable Men also "own" Sheriff Barnes and influence local law enforcement. Early in the novel, they skillfully manipulate the handling of Armstrong Todd's murder and the trial of Floyd Cox. Although annoyed by the brutish violence of the poor white men, they have little remorse for the black child's life or the grieving community he left behind. They make sure that Floyd Cox serves some jail time while awaiting trial to appease national outrage and northern business interests. But as the Honorable Men have orchestrated, Floyd is ultimately acquitted for the murder. Campbell narrates:

> The Honorable Men of Hopewell had blood on their hands. Since the days of the New Deal they had manipulated relief benefits so that poor whites were often denied payments and pushed out of the county in order to keep in blacks who would work for starvation wages. . . . And now they were going to decide the fates of the men who murdered Armstrong.[25]

Under Stonewall's direction, they decide to create the spectacle of justice with an arrest of the Cox men and a trial for Floyd Cox. They proceed in this course of action with the clear knowledge that the white man would not be convicted for such a crime. Here enters Campbell's commentary on class politics among a rural white citizenry. However despicable they think Floyd is, they also understand that he is white and therefore cannot be heavily punished for the death of a black person. The Honorable Men try unsuccessfully to minimize any upheaval and attention around the violent tragedy. While the wealthy white upper class is not depicted as outwardly violent or as hostile as poor, uneducated whites, they have no value for black life. Nonetheless, they rank wealth and class above their alliance with poor whites. Stonewall's character functions as a symbol of rich, white "good ol' boys" of the South. He and the Honorable Men are a metaphor for the thinly veiled racism and facade of civility purported to conceal the destructive institutional bigotry that, while less overt than lynching and violence, is just as insidious.

In *Your Blues* Campbell complicates white racism and privilege, while giving a humanistic view and personal face to the individuals grappling with their responsibility for and complicity with white oppression and racial violence. She demonstrates an acute racial consciousness and political awareness that explores the tenuous nature of black/white racial politics in the United States across time and region. Clayton Pinochet is head of the newspaper and son of the wealthy landowner, Stonewall Pinochet. He represents the next generation of white privilege and power in Hopewell, Mississippi, but he is ambivalent about how to wield his influence. Clayton was also a tutor for the slain teen, Armstrong, who helped out around his office. Torn by the death of his young protégé, Clayton secretly alerts northern news media of the tragedy, inviting them to cover the murder trial. Clayton also holds an affinity for the black community in Hopewell and frequently offered assistance to residents of the Quarters (the segregated section of town). This sympathy stems back to his childhood and his love for his primary caregiver (mammy), a black female employee named Etta. Clayton also recalls being a small child watching his father beat a black employee and Stonewall's violent response:

> Even now he could taste his eight-year-old passion. "Stop it! It's not right!" he screamed, flinging his small body between the two men. Suddenly he was lifted up, and then he was momentarily airborne, before he landed on the ground with a thud. When he looked up, his father's body loomed over him. Stonewall Pinochet's face was contorted with rage and venom as he shouted, "If you ever—ever—try to save a nigger again, I'll . . ." He stalked away.[26]

This moment marked Clayton's deep compassion for black people as well as his entrenched fear of his father. As a result, his help would always be accompanied by doubtfulness, reluctance, and discretion.

An anomaly among the wealthy whites of his father's generation, Clayton Pinochet represents Campbell's critique of the kindhearted white liberal whose timidity becomes a betrayal to black allies, or, at best, an incapacity to assist in social and economic improvement for black people in Hopewell. Clayton Pinochet has a strong aversion to the ways of his wealthy white father and the other elite ruling class of whites in Hopewell. Despite his distaste for the power brokering and white racism of the South, Clayton possesses an overwhelming cowardice that waters down his kindness toward blacks and his passion for his well-kept black mistress, Marguerite. In another scene Clayton gives audience to the angry racism of a waitress in the local diner.

> Florine hissed, slamming down Clayton's lunch so hard his steak bounced in the air in front of him. Clayton watched as her chest heaved in and out, every breath an angry explosion that reddened her face and further strained her soiled uniform. . . . "Why would anybody want to write something in the newspaper about a nigger anyway?"[27]

He imagines his response where he is freed of his fears:

> He wanted . . . to say to Florine that he believed that negroes were human beings and deserved better than being murdered by trash like the Coxes. He wanted to stand on top of the table and hurl his plate of steaming chicken-fried steak across the counter and tell all the customers in the café, as they picked globs of mashed potatoes from their eyes and hair, that he, Clayton Pinochet, had called in the Yankees and was glad that they were here with their notepads and pencils, their cameras and flash bulbs, and hoped that more would come, because it was time that the entire country learned about the barbaric cannibalism that was eating them all alive.[28]

But Clayton fails to respond at all:

> A scream was burning through his throat like whiskey. Of course, as usual he remained silent. He could make a telephone call in the dark, he couldn't make a public statement. Strong words could lead to repercussions. . . . One day he would speak out. One day he would save black people, lead them out of their own misery. But not today.[29]

Although he does not share the sentiments of most whites in Hopewell, Clayton must ultimately reconcile his useless paternalism and make amends for his silence on the racist ways of his rural Mississippi town. Having found emotional solace in his relationships with black people as early as his caregiver, Etta, and later with his mentee, Armstrong, and his mistress, Marguerite, he reveals a selfish and cathartic interest in the black community. His affair with Marguerite also buffered his feelings of guilt about his white privilege and his father's reign over Hopewell's politics. However, Clayton Pinochet, although he struggles and fails repeatedly, has the most potential to help or at least do no harm, but it requires major sacrifice, insistence from others, and in some cases flat-out ultimatums. Consequently, he must also resolve his personal demons and fears to sustain a more genuine alliance with blacks in Hopewell. Campbell writes Clayton in contrast to the old guard of his father and his contemporaries; Clayton's character challenges the idea of "good whites" and exposes the problem of white liberal sentiments. While secretly despising the hostility and exploitation of blacks in the South, Clayton sidesteps confrontation with the structural problems of Hopewell. Appreciated for his kindness and assistance to the black community, Clayton fails to challenge other white men—neither his father nor the Coxes—and thus is complicit in the racist violence and terror that plague this small community.

The poor and working-class whites in Hopewell reflect another layer to the racial dynamics of the small town. Husband and wife Floyd and Lily Cox have their two children, Doreen and Floyd-junior. Floyd's parents (Mamie and Lester) live nearby, along with his older brother, John Earl, who is more successful than Floyd and also has a family of his own. The following description of the novel's setting best situates the material differences between wealthy and poor whites and black workers in the Hopewell community:

> They [Floyd and Lily] walked to his brother's home, passing houses that resembled their own: shotgun clapboards set up on cinder blocks, where the gardens were haphazard affairs and the chickens and guineas where likely to wander into the front yard and even into the road. The string of homes owned by poor whites in the area faced a long stretch of hedges. Behind the hedges was a dump and in the back of that, the Quarters, a compound of rented two-room tarpaper shacks where the field hands and sharecroppers who worked the nearby

plantations lived. . . . Heading for town, driving across land that was perfectly flat, punctuated only by acres and acres of Pinochet cotton . . . [at] the city limits of Hopewell they could see the banks of the Yabulusha, which washed up along the east side of the delta town near the railroad track.[30]

Campbell uses the Cox family to suggest that possessing white skin privilege without the accompanying financial comfort and accoutrements of the wealthy elite can create a dangerous mix of anger, resentment, white loyalty, and racialized violence. For Floyd and his family, this frustrated sense of powerlessness and a desire for control is taken out on vulnerable black individuals whose lives mean little in rural 1950s Mississippi. Floyd's father and brother—hardworking, uneducated laborers—are a stark contrast to white men like the Pinochets. Although he owns the tiny pool shack for local blacks, Floyd isn't nearly the enterprising businessman that Stonewall Pinochet is, and he will never achieve a fraction of his success. While he is acquitted for Armstrong's murder in a quick trial, Floyd is seen as expendable by the Honorable Men of Hopewell, who write him off after he falls into poverty and lands in and out of jail for stealing and petty crimes.

Floyd lives a miserable existence as a result of his cowardly aggression against the defenseless young Armstrong. His unfortunate and failed attempt to impress and win approval from his father and brother ends up costing him everything. The author tells us:

Later when Floyd would try to forget everything else about this night, he would still recall the ride back home, the smoky air of the congested cab, the three of them pressed in close together, singing and laughing as their shoulders touched. What warmed him more than anything was the sure, true knowing that his father, at last, was satisfied with him.[31]

Later, Floyd's cowardice with the other Cox men is taken out on his family, and his hopelessness and rage transform to violent domestic abuse of his wife, Lily, and periodic abandonment of his family. Lily and Floyd Cox suffer financially after his acquittal of Armstrong's murder. Floyd and his family fall into poverty as his black patrons refuse to return to his small pool shack and he must close it down. He is unable to find work because of his reputation following the murder trial and because he is a poor, uneducated white man in rural Mississippi. He is in and out of jail, leaving his family neglected and near starving. Lily slowly begins to understand the hopelessness of her situation and struggles to raise her children alone while also enduring abuse from her husband's family and regular battering from Floyd himself. She realizes her husband is a man she thought had killed someone out of his love for her, but in fact only acted for the approval and acceptance of other white men. Floyd's experience as a poor white man who is powerless in all other arenas directly relates to Lily, and his role shifts from controlling head of household to violent abuser.

For the white men in the novel, rich or poor, women serve as simply another possession or object. For the poor Cox men, a wife was a most prized possession—especially given the absence of the lucrative business and financial holdings that the Pinochet men possessed. The class distinction between rich and powerful white men and poor working-class white men also undergirds the latter's fervent belief in superiority over black people and white women, thus wielding power in more severe ways. Lily Cox is the first character we meet in the novel, and she begins as the naive young wife of Floyd Cox, a poor white laborer. Lily, a former beauty queen, is initially unconscious of her own white privilege as she tries to negotiate her coddled place as bride and trophy-wife for Floyd. Campbell opens the first chapter of the novel with Lily listening to black sharecroppers singing as they work the fields of white landowners. She perceives these melodic work songs as a personal blessing and possession of her own. Lily's character is written with empathy, but she is not exonerated for her hand in Armstrong's death. A rural beauty, crowned Magnolia Queen at her high school, Lily grew up watching her mother suffer physical abuse from her father. Her mother excused her husband's violence and also looked the other way when young Lily confessed that her uncle had been sexually abusing her. She marries Floyd at age sixteen and quits high school despite appeals from an English teacher who sees Lily's intellectual potential. Lily longs for a life of beauty and extravagance and enjoys taking in the grandeur of rich homes and neighborhoods near the center of town:

> On these streets, half hidden behind a bank of towering magnolias, were large brick two-story homes with screened-in front porches and meticulous lawns where the shiny black faces of sculpted jockeys in red jackets and white pants were frozen in perpetual grins while inside, their living counterparts were equally accommodating. Lily often daydreamed about how it would be to live in one of these houses, the finest she'd ever seen. Of course, the sprawling plantation mansions of the Settles and Pinochets, reminiscent of the antebellum splendor that was part of the region's mythology, were grander. But who could even begin to imagine living in one of those?[32]

Lily's disillusionment over her life with Floyd ushers a thirst for something new or different, something to stimulate her curiosity:

> Lily didn't come into town very often and the sight of paved streets and the stores made her eyes open wide with expectation, even though the city was small, its business district not more than three or four blocks sandwiched between the two gins—both owned by the Pinochets—that made up the north and south boundaries. As they drove down Jefferson Davis Boulevard, the main downtown thoroughfare, she craned her neck in hopes of glimpsing the Chinaman who ran the town's laundry and the Chinese restaurant. Or maybe the Jew who owned the small department store would pass by. She yearned for something wild to touch, see, or feel. Some excitement.[33]

Lily is neither overtly nor violently racist and, as a poor, undereducated white woman, has her own history of abuse. She seems to have no sense of power within the patriarchal norms of the South. But the symbol of her white female position and her desire for something interesting is the catalyst for Armstrong's death. By peeking into her husband's pool hall to glimpse the black patrons, Lily sets into place the events leading to Armstrong's murder. She hears Armstrong speaking "exotic" French words to the pool hall regulars and smiles at him. Later she acknowledges to Ida that the young boy did not "talk fresh" to her as so accused.

> "Ida" she said leaning against her friend, "I gotta tell you something. Somebody told my husband that this colored boy was—uh, said something fresh to me today. But he didn't. I told my husband that. And everything's alright now. It's just I been a little upset, that's all. . . . Everything is all right. I told my husband, 'That boy didn't say not one bad thing.' Everything is alright now. I'm just a little upset. That's all."[34]

But her denial about the violence that ensues on her behalf and the dishonest court testimony she offers for her husband's acquittal places her in collusion with the Cox men responsible for Armstrong's death. Furthermore, the satisfaction and esteem she later finds in the perception that "[her] man would kill for [her]" add insult to injury. Clearly, Lily did not pull the trigger and as a woman was entrapped in the role prescribed for her, but Campbell questions whether this makes her any less responsible. Lily grapples with her responsibility and lack of power as she and the other white women in the Cox family watch their men go off in search of Armstrong:

> Lily wanted to call after them and say, "Ain't nothing happen with that boy," but one look at Mamie's stern, intractable face, at Louetta's accusing eyes, and she shut her mouth. If Floyd and them were gonna do something crazy and ruinous, she couldn't stop them. . . . The older woman's words sizzled. "Whatever they does is menfolk business. Us women ain't got nary to do with it." . . . Lily tried not to think about Floyd, Lester, and John Earl and what they might be doing together that night. She had felt happy and exhilarated sneaking into the poolhall, like a child stealing cookies that were cooling on the porch, but now she felt guilty, and frightened for the boy and herself.[35]

Through Lily we also see how patriarchy manifests as a part of white male racial identity, thus entangling the woman in a perilous web of helplessness, victimhood, and complicity.

In her years as a student activist at the University of Pitts-burgh, Campbell and her classmates initiated space in the group BWFBM in order to unpack the intricate racial and sexual poli-tics that manifest between white women and black men. As the campus integrated, some white female students engaged in the harassment and alienation of the black female students in their residence halls, and also began to explore their curiosity about black men, creating tension within the campus dating scene. Similar to her student activism, Campbell uses her fictional work, and Lily's character specifically, to comment on the sexual politics that function within white racism. Lily's character also suggests that white identity and skin privilege perpetuate social inequity that manifests in forms other than racial violence. Lily, even in her poverty, embodies "the cult of true womanhood" in which white women are placed on pedestals of virtue, feminin-ity, piety, and submissiveness.[36] This pedestal, which in truth was a constrictive framework for all women, left black women marginalized, devalued, and open to abuse and dehumaniza-tion. The cult of true womanhood included poor white women, but beauty and fragility also subjected them to silencing and abuse, as we see in Lily's case. In addition, Campbell shows how this cult of true womanhood was the precipitator for the "justified" violence and lynching of black men. In an interview, Campbell describes a time in history when the mere accusation of dishonoring the virtue of a white woman by a black man was cause for lynching:

> In the American South . . . the subjugation of white women and the
> harsh active racism went hand in hand. White women were the excuse
> in many instances for the acting out of racism's harshest punishment
> to preserve and protect white womanhood. Black men were lynched,
> and so many of the times they were lynched is directly because they
> were accused of raping white women or indirectly because they chal-
> lenged white authority in a way that would move them closer to being
> a sexual threat to white men. [For example] opening up a store that
> competed with a white man that put them in a position to earn more,
> which put them in a position to be more attractive to white females.[37]

Rape accusations were often fabricated and worked to control black men seen as social or economic threats (that is, those with money, education, land, or businesses).[38] Armstrong and Lily's interaction is framed in this context, as is the reaction from Floyd, his family, and the white citizens of Hopewell in general. This troublesome matrix of race, class, sex, and violence—which would continue throughout history—gets exposed in the white characters of *Your Blues*, as they react and respond to social position, power, and powerlessness, and control over black people and white women.

The importance of Bebe Moore Campbell's characterizations in *Your Blues Ain't Like Mine* is that she offers complexity beyond good/bad or racist/not racist with respect to white racial identity. She instead explores how various individuals and groups wield white privilege and engage in or challenge racial terror, inequity, and prejudice. While the Honorable Men of Hopewell have a long history of oppressing and disenfranchising the black community, the Cox family spews and perpetuates racist rhetoric and racial stereotypes as a normal practice and belief. However, the Coxes have little social or economic power and do not experience power until they become violent and terrorize Armstrong. Thus Campbell provides us with a closer examination of relationships between white poverty and violence, and white wealth and socio-economic oppression. From these characters we gain an intimate portrayal of social class and family relations that sustain privilege, racial violence, bigotry, and institutional racism. Most important, she complicates the idea that "all white people are the same" and provides an interesting critique of would-be allies, sympathizers, and friends, like Clayton and Lily.

Campbell writes Lily's positionality with empathy and honesty. The white woman is both understood in her humanity, fallibility, and life station and simultaneously exposed for her mistakes that become a matter of life and death for Armstrong Todd. Although her immaturity and naïveté eventually fall away, her life becomes very difficult and painful, and she continues to be abused by men. She is curious about black people and desires Ida's friendship. Still, as often was the case in the socialization of white women,

Lily did not act outside of her prescribed role. She does not find the voice either to speak against the atrocities of her own people or to save the life of an innocent black child. It is only with the passing of time and her daughter Doreen's fearlessness that Lily begins to find her voice as a white woman in the rural South.

While Floyd and Stonewall exist at two ends of the spectrum in the quest for oppressive white male power and dominance, Lily and Clayton represent a potentially kind white person with an attachment to, interest in, or affinity for black communities. In many cases their warm sentiment and the absence of malice would suffice to distinguish them from Floyd and Stonewall. However, Lily's helplessness and Clayton's cowardice impede their ability to become true allies or advocates of their black neighbors. Furthermore, both of them have some level of self-interest and unconsciously associate black identity with an unmet need—independence and strength for Lily, and safety and solace for Clayton. Throughout much of the novel, Clayton and Lily lack bravery and confidence; thus they are politically useless and burdensome to the black community from this position. This fear of risk that many whites struggle to overcome makes them of little use in the struggle for social justice and civil rights. As we see in Hopewell, the black citizens are eventually able to take up the fight and champion their own causes, for better life and working conditions.

As Campbell reveals the reluctance (and sometimes inability) of these characters to challenge the systemic nature of racism or to directly address the white people in their families and communities, their responsibility, agency, and resistance can be better understood. Campbell's care in writing these characters is not meant to excuse the destructive nature of racism but to offer a humanistic and diverse representation of white people (to themselves and to nonwhites). She challenges misperceptions that racism is only perpetuated by a few hate-spewing bigots "who just haven't progressed" with the greater mass of liberal white people. Campbell's treatment of white racism and patriarchy reflects her time at the University of Pittsburgh and the black political discourse of the period. Confronting racial violence and critiquing white supremacy directly connect to the racial consciousness of the BAS. Additionally, during that period she and coauthor Martha Carson, in the pamphlet *Black Students Seize the Power to Define*, write about progressive gender roles for black men and women and call for black men to reject aspirations for white patriarchy and models of masculinity.[39] But twenty years later when *Your Blues* is published, Campbell exacts a more sophisticated analysis of race, gender, and white identity. Her white characters are fully developed; each depiction is, at once, humane, complex, sympathetic, and gruesome. More important, she reveals how these white characters are connected to black people, complicit in history's violence, and, in some cases, redeemable. She integrates a class and gendered analysis that extends beyond the leading ideas of black nationalism that reflects aspects of DuBoisian Marxism[40] as well as black feminist thought that was emerging in the 1970s when she left Pitt. When asked about the troubles of her black and white and male and female characters in relation to the novel's title, Campbell offers:

> I meant for the title to be ironic because I feel sometimes our blues are equally as hard as the other person's. I certainly feel that our blues are intertwined. In other words, Lily's blues of being a subjugated, molested, white baby girl directly feed into Armstrong Todd's blues of being a murdered black boy which feeds into his mother's blues which feeds into Clayton Pinochet's blues of being a helpless white male. So it goes back and forth.[41]

As they age, Clayton and Lily do begin to change. In Marguerite's absence, Clayton is able to grow and forge a healthy platonic relationship with Ida Long as the two collaborate to tutor and educate black youth in the area. Clayton is left alone to grapple with his demons as he mourns Marguerite's departure. Lily leaves Floyd eventually, and she begins to heal from years of abuse. Through her daughter, Doreen, and small granddaughter she learns about agency, female independence and interdependence, and, most of all, love.

The final important and recurring feature of Bebe Moore Campbell's writing found in *Your Blues* is the thematic use of forgiveness, healing, and redemption as the plot resolution. While she doesn't offer predictable endings, her work usually culminates with some sort of humanistic reconciliation. Her characters never "walk off into the sunset" to live happily ever after. Instead, there is a denouement where several crises are resolved at once or in close proximity and the causal roots remain as ongoing personal work for the characters. Although she doesn't depict completion of this self-work, the allusion implies hopefulness, and the characters experience forgiveness and a sense of personal agency. In the novel, forgiveness is granted for both small trespasses to the most forsaken offenses—betrayal, abandonment, and even murder. But the forgiveness is intended for the self-healing and release of one's own trauma (that is, Delotha and Ida). Campbell's use of forgiveness does not free the obvious offenders like Lily, Floyd, Wydell, or Stonewall from responsibility. But instead of vengeful retribution, forgiveness requires taking ownership of one's responsibility and accepting the consequences of his or her actions. By positioning forgiveness as a form of reconciliation and restorative justice, Campbell enacts the final stage of the frame-shifting process, which is *frame transformation*. At the transformation stage, frames or value positions are shifted substantially, helping individuals to challenge their deeply held beliefs.[42]

In *Your Blues* Campbell crafts an intricate web of reconciliation for the Cox family, with Lily's daughter, Doreen, serving as a symbol of generational change. As the catalyst and symbolic reason for Armstrong's murder, Lily suffers immensely in the years following Floyd's acquittal. She doesn't "get over it" or go on peacefully with her life. While Floyd is serving time for robbery, Lily's roof caves in, and she and her children move in with Mamie. She goes to apply for welfare and is pressured into performing oral sex on the caseworker to get assistance. After Lily has an emotional meltdown at the local store, her sister-in-law returns for a visit and shares her sedative medication with Lily. Lily is hospitalized shortly afterward for a nervous breakdown. When Lily recovers, she returns to Floyd and his violent beatings. The two develop an increasing resentment of black people as they observe the national progression of civil rights and contrast it to the poverty and misery in their own lives. As a young teen, tired of seeing her father abuse her mother, Doreen defends Lily against her father's violence and threatens to harm Floyd if his battering continues. In this act she bucks against patriarchal domestic violence and also demonstrates a sense of courage that her mother has never been able to access. Enduring the abuse for several more years, Lily eventually leaves Floyd. When Lily tries to rationalize Floyd's abuse and a woman's place, her daughter, Doreen, gets upset:

> "That's bullshit, Mama," Doreen said, and she instantly regret-
> ted the harshness in her voice; her mother looked as though she'd
> been slapped. She said gently, "Hasn't he made your life a living hell
> already? All that meanness he got inside of him, all that ugliness he
> can't control. What do you think he's gon' do with it? He will kill you.
> Just like he done that boy." She could see her mother struggling with
> the twin fears: of being with her father and of being alone.[43]

Lily moves in with an adult Doreen, who works as a laborer at the New Plantation Catfish Farm and Processing Plant. Doreen is a divorced mother living independently in her trailer home after experiencing domestic violence in her own marriage. Lily also notices her daughter's shifting racial consciousness. Lily's man-ufactured distance from blacks in Hopewell and her immature understanding of race relations are challenged (as is the general prejudice common to poor whites in the South) as Doreen works side by side with local blacks at New Plantation. Doreen even begins to develop kinships and alliances as she joins forces with a middle-aged Ida protesting the harsh work conditions and low wages at the factory. Doreen's fiery spirit and self-efficacy amazes Lily, but she is also very proud of her daughter and begins to fancy her own growth as well. Doreen also surpasses Lily's maturity on racial acceptance. With the improved conditions, increased vis-ibility in TV and media, and experience of an integrated work setting, Doreen releases her parents' fear, anxiety, and bigotry toward black people, and struggles alongside her black colleagues based on their shared struggle as poor workers. As she takes her own daughter with her to a protest, Doreen tells her mother:

> "No, I don't know what's gonna happen, but I'll tell you what: no matter what happens, I want her to know that she has to stand up for herself. 'Cause if she don't, won't nobody do it for her. I want her to have courage." Lily's eyes almost met her daughter's but at the last moment she looked away. Courage was what men were supposed to have: that was what she wanted to say. But the words froze on her lips. "Y'all be careful," she whispered.[44]

Not only does Doreen discard the racial hatred passed down in her family, she also strives to be a brave and self-determined woman. Her self-assuredness breaks the cycle that trapped her mother, Lily.

In the closing scene of the final chapter, Campbell foreshadows the beginning steps of resolution and healing for Armstrong's father, Wydell. Wydell, who struggles with the wounds of growing up as a black man in 1930s Mississippi, is particularly anxious about raising another son after his initial abandonment of Delotha and Armstrong, so much so that he is unable to rise to the challenge of parenting WT. After several failed attempts to nurture a relationship with WT and harsh rejection from Delotha, Wydell gives up and resumes drinking after almost twenty years of sobriety. On the night that WT disappears with a gun, his cousin, Lionel, finds the demoralized father in a bar and presses him to step up. They head out to a coffee shop where Wydell sobers up and then goes to look for WT. WT has been hanging out with friends, and a skirmish ensues, leaving him running from gunshots. Wydell finds WT before the police or other gangbangers. He takes his son on a trip down south—toward Hopewell and toward healing. The ride begins with a minor confrontation between the father and son. WT sleeps for much of the ride, shaken by his sobering near-death experience. When he awakes, he and Wydell gradually begin to talk. Wydell takes a risk and presses past his feelings of intimidation and past WT's repugnant attitude. He acknowledges his alcoholism and the need to stop drinking, and tells his son of rural Mississippi where he and Delotha grew up. He tells WT about how Delotha and he survived the harsh conditions by singing as they worked in the fields. He explains to WT the importance of understanding their history, where his people came from, and where his brother Armstrong was murdered. But Wydell, who hasn't returned south since his youth, needs to see the place as well. The return will allow him to face his demons, the wounds that caused his alcoholism, and the loss of his first-born son. Hopewell has changed significantly in forty years, and with WT at his side, Wydell possesses the potential to begin his own healing and to recover their relationship as well.

Campbell uses this father-son relationship and WT's troubled character to resurrect the lynched black boys of the South, like the fictional Armstrong Todd and the real-life Emmett Till, and connect them to the many sons and brothers lost in urban violence and gang activity in the North. WT's life has been spared, giving both him and his parents an opportunity to forgive, grow, and correct mistakes of the past. This familial shift happens simultaneous to the political changes of 1980s Hopewell and the protests at the Catfish Plantation. It is no coincidence that after Armstrong's death, Ida Long's son, Sweetbabe, is able to live and thrive in Hopewell as a young black male. Sweetbabe is seemingly of minor significance, but after being tutored by Clayton and heading to Chicago for better opportunities, the young man actually decides to return to Hopewell to teach in the black community. His ability to survive the racist South as a young black male and his surprising affinity for his hometown are a testament to the collective change of the community in Hopewell.

After about twenty years, Ida's activist spirit eventually wins improved conditions by organizing workers at New Plantation. This offers a greater sense of self-worth and determination for her community, but also unifies poor whites and blacks under a shared cause. Ida's activism is evidenced early on in her refusal to accept low-quality schooling for black children. She collaborates with Clayton Pinochet to tutor and run an educational program serving youth in the Quarters. She also spearheads protests and legal action against the town of Hopewell for discrimination at a local senior citizens center. In many ways, her character functions as a vehicle through the history of southern black experience across four decades, thus allowing readers to engage the personal experience and impact of historical and cultural shifts in recent US history. Despite her lost dreams of moving north to Chicago, Ida emerges as a major activist, leader, and change agent in Hopewell.

Campbell seems to write the middle-aged Ida in a similar spirit of the character Willow Scott in terms of her boldness, but Ida also forges her own path and cultivates institutional and social change in Hopewell through organizing and direct action. Campbell uses her characters to affirm women as competent and strategic leaders capable of initiating and sustaining a movement. Ida becomes a *bridge leader* in her own right. Ida experiences multiple losses but recovers and "keeps living," as Willow advised her in her youth. She differs from Delotha because she is able to reconcile her pain and disappointment rather than become paralyzed by it. Her persistence and success in educating her son, Sweetbabe, fuel her desire to improve lives for others in Hopewell. Her alliances with Doreen Cox and Clayton Pinochet reveal her ability to both inspire and cajole, crossing racial lines and showing others their personal power and agency. Ida coaxes Clayton out of his self-pity about losing Marguerite by encouraging him to channel his energy elsewhere and using his talent to start an education program for black children. He is reluctant at first, and she volunteers to work as his aide. Clayton quickly realizes that he finds this work quite satisfying, and ultimately he is able to do real and sustained service in the black community.

Ida's relationship with Clayton Pinochet offers another site of healing within the novel. These unlikely allies are brought together once more in the most unexpected of ways. Ida's early experiences with Clayton's benevolence include his help at the time of Armstrong's death and then again when Ida's small son, Sweetbabe, is bitten by a rabid dog and he takes them to a white doctor for medical help. About a decade later Ida presses him again, this time to tutor her son the way he had done with his protégé, Armstrong

Todd. Sweetbabe is about the same age at this time as Armstrong was when he was slain, but struggles more as a student because of the subpar segregated education he receives in the South. These moments collectively form a tentative friendship between the two that is platonic in nature. Eventually Ida, who gave up her dreams of leaving Hopewell to tend to her ailing stepfather, William, discovers a long-kept secret when the old man passes away. In sorting through his things Ida discovers a box of keepsakes that belonged to her mother. Inside the box she finds letters and photographs of her as a baby, with her mother and a white man who is none other than the racist landowner Stonewall Pinochet. This discovery is uncanny given Stonewall's disdain for blacks, his hostility about Clayton's black mistress, and his intolerance of his son's affinity and benevolence to black Hopewell. As fate would have it, Ida's mother was a maid for the Pinochet family and a mistress to Stonewall. Ida keeps this information to herself at first, and doesn't tell Clayton that they are siblings. When Ida does finally share this information with Clayton, he is shocked as he remembers her mother Susie, the pretty young black woman who worked in his parents' home. His reverie is interrupted by Ida's appeal for inheritance that she warrants as Stonewall's daughter. Parting with some of his wealth is sobering to Clayton, and tension ensues. He threatens to defeat her in court when she asks for rights to the Pinochet estate. After some time passes, Clayton returns to Ida realizing that he values their relationship more than his long-awaited inheritance. Ida receives a generous settlement, and the two begin a more intimate relationship as siblings and friends. Clayton overcomes his fear of confronting white privilege and institutional oppression. By the end of the novel he joins the protest demonstration at the New Plantation Catfish Farm and Processing Plant. His inheritance of Stonewall's estate, land, and financial holdings also foreshadows a new era in Hopewell.

In *Your Blues* Armstrong's violent murder and the exploitative grip of racism are gradually reconciled on both the personal and systemic levels. Healing occurs first in generational shifts. Doreen, a poor and working-class white woman, chooses to think and act differently than her parents, and creates a life that she can be proud of and satisfied with. Sweetbabe, with Clayton's and Ida's support, finds value in the rural town of Hopewell and experiences the South differently than Armstrong. Even the impertinent WT has the opportunity to reclaim his future and his relationship with his father. Of course the shifting US social landscape from the 1950s to the late 1980s ushers in much of this change, so that the passing of time and the coming of the next generation offer the chance to forgive and to heal the pain and loss of the past. Reconciliation also occurs through collective action such that Ida's community organizing creates opportunities for interracial and cross-generational alliances in Hopewell. Ida's collaborative leadership yields changes in the quality of life for Hopewell's black and white citizens and creates many new opportunities. Finally, the personal growth that many of the characters find implies a spiritual quality to Campbell's commentary. There is an emphasis on forgiveness and surrendering negative emotions like guilt, hatred, resentment, and fear. Campbell effectively accounts for all major and minor characters, and there is also hinting at Delotha's healing as well. As she finally seeks help finding WT in Wydell Sr.'s absence, she begins to cry and acknowledge the multiple layers of hurt she carries:

> She wiped her eyes as she dressed. If anyone had asked her, she would have said she was crying for a lot of reasons, for a lot of people, but at the moment she couldn't put any of those reasons into words. All she knew was that she had to find Wydell.[45]

Campbell writes some of the more venomous characters out with old age and death (Stonewall Pinochet, Lester and John Earl Cox); however, she allows Floyd, Armstrong's murderer, to continue living. It is unclear whether she keeps him alive as if some redemption or reckoning is possible, or simply for him to suffer the guilt and misery that remains of his offenses. This suggests that some aspects of racism die out and some aspects continue to live on. Ultimately, Campbell uses the "blues" as a metaphor for the differential racial experiences of her characters and each one's journey through his or her personal blues. In her own words about writing this book, she says:

I think it taught me that my capacity to be generous to characters on a page is only an introduction to my capacity for healing and forgiveness in real life. And I still, as a human being, have a lot of work to do in that area.[46]

And likewise for her characters, she offers this explanation:

Well, I wanted to end it with the realization that there is hard work that still has to be done. The hard work of Wydell going on a twelve-step program to shake his addiction. The hard work of his son WT stepping away from delinquency and becoming a responsible adult. The responsibility of helping that young man shape his life was Wydell's; the responsibility of putting the family back together. So there's a lot of work to be done. A lot of hope that it could be done, because the tools were in place. . . . Well if singing a song is what got you through then do that. "That" being symbolic of more than music but of religion, belief in a greater power, all those things. Do those things that will make you whole. Attempt to do those things that will make you whole.[47]

Here we see Campbell's effective use of frame shifting as she begins with a narrative about lynching and segregation, but weaves in broader issues relevant to readers across race, gender, and class lines. This illustrates the move from *frame bridging*, in which she shares historical information, and *frame amplification*, which connects this information to the reader's existing values and concern, to *frame extension*, the incorporation of related social concerns. Campbell resolves the novel with the urging forth of personal growth, healing, and forgiveness. In doing so, she demonstrates the activist process of *frame transformation* by challenging the spirit of collective resentment and retaliation for racial violence with a radically different response. As a child of the black liberation era and nurtured with a black nationalist ethic during her college years, Campbell moves in a completely different direction. The idea of personal healing and forgiveness is radical but seemingly counterintuitive to the idea of taking a stand and confronting oppressive structures and policies. The concept of peaceful reconciliation, whether internally or between two opposing entities, is a conceptual shift that she challenges her readers, along with her characters, to make. By way of the framing process, Campbell draws in readers, connects to important issues like racial violence, and widens the scope of concern to include related social political concerns (such as gendered and socioeconomic inequities). At the close of the novel, she offers completely new and radical ways to think about and resolve social problems through personal transformation, relationship building, and community organizing.

In a narrative that moves across three-and-a-half decades, *Your Blues Ain't Like Mine* weaves together the hearts and lives of blacks and whites in a small community turned upside down by its racial tension and the cold-blooded murder of an innocent black child. *Your Blues* is especially valuable for popular audiences and fiction-readers because it bridges recent African American historical experience to contemporary social issues. The novel also effectively elucidates complex political ideas so that readers can relate to and understand the experiences, identities, and social position of the characters. Campbell uses her writing as a vehicle for difficult dialogues about race and violence by connecting her commentary to familiar and accessible narratives of family, relationships, and personal transformation.

While there is obvious maturation from age twenty-one when Campbell graduates from the University of Pittsburgh to age forty-two when *Your Blues Ain't Like Mine* is published, there is resounding consistency in the sociopolitical issues with which Campbell is concerned. From her writings about gender as a student there is surely an evolution that takes place. We see that, as Campbell matures, she yields a more exact articulation of African American history and culture, and precise commentary on racial violence, interracial interactions, and gender and sexuality. As she ages and matures she articulates the additional importance of reconciliation, healing, and forgiveness—spiritual principles that were not the primary tenets of black nationalist discourse of her college years but still resonated as necessary to Campbell. As her career and life move forward, we find these commitments to be consistent in her future writing and activist work as she explores new sociopolitical concerns and issues. As her first novel, *Your Blues Ain't Like Mine* won Campbell great acclaim and earned her prominence and popularity within the literacy scene during the 1990s. She would continue to satisfy readers and critics with subsequent novels written with a similar style, thematic structure, and sociopolitical commentary.

The final chapter explores Campbell's final novel, *72 Hour Hold*, and its recurrent themes, while focusing on the sociopolitical commentary and implications of this fictional account. This book, based on her personal experience as a mother, became recommended reading for families within the National Alliance on Mental Illness. The fictional narrative offers a deeper understanding of the life turns, difficulties, and transformation in the face of mental illness.

# From Podium to Pen and Paper: *72 Hour Hold* as Commentary, Critique, and Catharsis

> *Writers are supposed to write what they know.*
> *And I know about mental illness.*
> —Bebe Moore Campbell, interview by Ashok Gangadean
> (*Global Lens*), February 5, 2006

The 2005 release of *72 Hour Hold* proved to be a perfect convergence of Bebe Moore Campbell's personal life, her activist work with NAMI Urban Los Angeles (NULA), and her professional life as a writer. Following the success of her first novel, *Your Blues Ain't Like Mine,* Campbell continued to write and publish. She received acclaim with her three subsequent novels, *Brothers and Sisters* (1994), *Singing in the Comeback Choir* (1998), and *What You Owe Me* (2001). Each of these works would continue to explore contemporary issues, African American life, relationships, family, and personal transformation. Many of her signature themes would recur in each novel. Campbell also sought balance in her personal life and cultivated healthy bonds with her family and friends, especially during times of hardship. Her mother, Doris Moore, would join her family in Los Angeles, relocating from Philadelphia, and by the late 1990s Campbell would eventually become a grandmother herself. Both events strengthened her familial commitments.[1] Additionally, in her multidimensional career, Campbell held a regular spot on National Public Radio (NPR) as a commentator on *Daily Edition*, and was a successful journalist and speaker.

After her fourth novel, *What You Owe Me* (2002), she published her first children's book, *Sometimes My Mommy Gets Angry* (2003), for children with a mentally ill and/or addicted parent. She also penned a play, *Even with the Madness* (2002), dealing with familial coping with mental illness, which she shared with NULA support groups.

In the novel *72 Hour Hold*, which would be her final major publication, Campbell advances the cause of mental health awareness, health care, and policy reform. The novel functions as a part of her activism and sociopolitical commentary by teaching the general reader about the intimate and everyday experiences of living with mental illness; critiquing the inefficacies and disparities in mental health care access, resources, and support; and theorizing the steps for healing, support, and acceptance while coping with family mental illness. Margo V. Perkins's analysis of autobiographical narrative in her work *Autobiography as Activism: Three Black Women of the Sixties* is useful for examining the unique fictional narrative in *72 Hour Hold*. Her study of autobiographies by Angela Davis, Assata Shakur, and Elaine Brown lends attention to the intellectual offerings embedded in personal narratives by black women. While Campbell's accounting in the novel is imaginative, she acknowledges that she has her own experience of a mentally ill loved one.[2] In a public address she admits:

> Writers are supposed to write what they know. And I know about mental illness. I have a mentally ill family member. And I saw the illness begin to be manifested about eight or nine years ago. And at that point I was shut down completely. Went right into denial. Allowed stigma to overtake me. I was ashamed and embarrassed. I didn't want to talk about it. I forbid anyone in the house to talk about it outside of the house.[3]

Campbell's proximity to the issue of mental health personalizes the first-person stance used to depict Keri, her main character. This can be likened to the autobiographical "I" that Perkins discusses and notes as both factual and fictive.[4] As a novelist, Campbell is similar to the women in Perkins's work (Shakur, Brown, and Davis) who use personal writing as a tool of activism. In *72 Hour Hold* she is at once supplanting pedagogy, criticism, and theory in the interest of a social issue that she finds important and to which she is committed.

In 72 Hour Hold Keri Whitmore is a divorced mother of eighteen-year-old Trina, who has been diagnosed with bipolar disorder[5] for just over a year. The two live in a mixed-income neighborhood in South Los Angeles (Crenshaw/Inglewood) circa the late 1990s/early 2000s. Keri owns a high-end consignment boutique, and formerly worked as publicist and as a massage therapist. Keri is anxious about Trina's illness and frustrated with the lack of support from her ex-husband, Clyde, as their daughter goes from compliant to noncompliant with her medication and support program. As Trina becomes a legal adult, Keri is no longer able to enforce medication, treatment, or hospitalization. The mother attends a parent support group meeting across town where she has found a new circle of friends whose family members have mental illness. In her shame, she avoids her old life, her old friends, and her ex-boyfriend, Orlando.

The novel, which is written in first person, provides a very intimate account of one mother's struggle for stability and acceptance of her daughter's illness. It also reveals the institutional inefficacies of the mental health system, the stigmas of mental illness, and the differential experiences of African Americans with mental illness. Campbell's character-driven focus in 72 Hour Hold captivates the reader with Keri's tumultuous journey toward acceptance and healing. Compared to the range of lead and secondary characters in Your Blues Ain't Like Mine, Keri, in 72 Hour Hold, emerges as the single most prominent figure who carries the novel forward. Still, Campbell surrounds Keri with a rich host of secondary characters who are important to the plot. Her family includes her daughter, Trina; her ex-husband, Clyde; her on-and-off boyfriend, Orlando; and her estranged mother, Emma. Keri has a support group of African American parents—Gloria, Mattie, and Milton—whose adult children also have mental illness. Other characters are introduced when a single white mother, Bethany, encourages Keri to take Trina's care into her own hands. The two women are assisted by Brad, Pete, and Cecilia as they try to get alternative help for their daughters.

The trends and themes of Campbell's first novel, *Your Blues*, emerge as a signature style wielded with mastery in her final novel, *72 Hour Hold*. The following sections of this chapter address each of Campbell's four signature themes. Racial commentary is addressed in the first section; African American historical memory is the focus of the second; black women's racialized gender experience is examined in the third; and forgiveness and reconciliation are the signature themes in the final section.

In recent years mental health awareness efforts have become increasingly visible as evidenced by the rise in care, advocacy organizations, public discourse, and positive representation depictions in the media and popular culture.[6] Through the novel *72 Hour Hold*, Campbell explores mental illness in narrative form, focusing on the issues specific to black communities. She offers direct and specific commentary on the current state of the mental health care systems and the personal experience within families, thus positing that mental illness is an important social issue deserving of serious attention and reform. The relationship between Keri and her daughter, Trina, is the most primary and obvious vehicle for this commentary. However, supporting characters and minor plots also help elucidate the stereotypes, stigmas, and problems that accompany the care of a loved one with mental illness.

Trina is hospitalized on multiple occasions, and these involuntary hospitalizations are known as seventy-two-hour holds. During a seventy-two-hour hold, a consumer (the person receiving mental health service) is held in a locked mental health facility for three days, or seventy-two hours, in order to stabilize and resume his or her treatment plan. While in the facility, patients receive stronger doses of medication and drug counseling, and participate in support groups. A seventy-two-hour hold is the customary procedure when a mentally ill person loses control and becomes harmful to himself or herself and others. After being held for three days, there is a hearing to determine if the stay needs to be extended or if the consumer is stable enough to be released. Keri's major problems with Trina begin just after her eighteenth birthday. The teen had been hospitalized three times after her senior year of high school, and Keri thought the strange behavior was due to drug use and stress. However, during the second stay Trina was diagnosed with bipolar disorder. After several months of stability and compliance with her medication and a daily counseling program that followed her third hold, Trina's behavior takes a peculiar shift. Keri suspects that she has gotten hold of some marijuana, a popular recreational drug among teens that, after its initial calming effect, can send a bipolar person into manic fits. She also believes that Trina has been "cheeking" her daily medication rather than actually swallowing it. Campbell's portrayal begins by examining the experiences of the consumer and parents or caregivers. The initial experience of diagnosis with mental illness and the subsequent coping is often a private and confusing process. Accepting the diagnosis is a large part of the difficulty, followed by feelings of conflict about having to detain one's child in a locked facility or to submit oneself to hospitalization.

In the novel, Trina's manic episodes included a spectrum of behavior ranging from abnormal to harmful. Initially, Trina was surly and noncommunicative with episodes of high-speed driving and expensive shopping sprees. Keri mistook this as typical teenage rebellion until Trina began cursing at her and waging verbal attacks. She would often call her mother "demon queen," "devil," and other paranoid and accusatory taunts. Furthermore, when Trina would go through these high-energy episodes, she might spend the entire night in a spell of overstimulation with the television and stereo blaring while making back-to-back local and long-distance phone calls to family members, friends, and acquaintances; or she might adorn herself in provocative clothing and wild garish makeup and take to the streets against her mother's wishes. Trina's episodes would eventually become physically aggressive, and she might shove or hit her mother or break things. Her third hospitalization occurred after she took a hammer and broke every window in the house and in her mother's car. After this last episode, and a stay in the county hospital, Trina commits to compliance and self-care, which stabilizes her until right around her eighteenth birthday. With this intimate narrative, Campbell offers an unfiltered portrait of mental health crises and the characteristics of a manic fit or mental health episode.

The explicit narration is an act of destigmatizing mental illness and "coming out of the closet" of shame that many families carry. Like Keri, many African American parents and families feel doubly ashamed and afraid of any blemish on their personal or familial image. For the reader who is unfamiliar with the experience of mental illness, the novel's descriptive nature is at once shocking, unsettling, and informative; alternatively, it will ring familiar and perhaps even painful for the reader who has grappled with the mental illness of a loved one.

Through her novel, Campbell is able to engage readers in an act of frame bridging that connects those with a general awareness of mental health issues, and especially those who have a personal experience with mental illness in their families. The intimate narrative connects the readers with the social issues that inspire the fictional account. Keri, who is obviously traumatized by this major upheaval in her life and her daughter's life, lives on eggshells hoping that Trina does not regress. She is very attentive and makes sure that Trina eats well and takes her antipsychotic medication and mood stabilizer each day. She also drops her off and picks her up from a partial day program for outpatient mental health at a prestigious medical center in Beverly Hills. When Trina begins to "play hooky" from the program, Keri ignores other signs, hopeful that her daughter remains stable. Trina becomes standoffish, and Keri thinks she smells marijuana outside their house. Trina has another late night episode, then sneaks out of the house to talk to a neighborhood vagrant. Keri finally accepts that something is wrong and seeks help from Trina's psychiatrist, psychologist, and program director, but to no avail. Eventually, Trina escalates at her group meeting, begins screaming at everyone, and hits another patient. She is placed on her fourth seventy-two-hour hold by the program director. However, this time she is eighteen years old, a legal adult, which completely changes the stakes for Keri. At this transition, Keri and Trina's narrative reveals not only the emotional impact of mental illness but also the challenges that stem from policy and procedures within the mental health care system.

During the fourth hospitalization, Keri is troubled to find out that now that Trina is eighteen she cannot be legally mandated to take her medication at home. Furthermore, when she inquires about any drugs in Trina's system, she is told that although Trina is covered by Keri's insurance, she has not been designated by her daughter to receive information about her medical condition. What is worse is that Trina's hold extension is denied, and she is released on her own before Keri arrives to pick her up. Trina disappears for two days with a young man she met in the mental health facility, and Keri has no recourse. Keri becomes frantic because she cannot report her missing until the minimum time has passed (three days). When Trina finally returns home from her rampage the episodes continue for weeks. Keri is repeatedly told that Trina is not severe or extreme enough to meet the criteria for another hold until she becomes physically harmful to herself or others. Keri becomes impatient with the reality that she must be in the most desperate and worst-case scenario to receive help, and she laments: "Doesn't meet the criteria. No slit wrists for her; no bullet wounds for me."[7] Trina eventually goes to live with her father, but soon after gets arrested for shoplifting. Keri cannot bail her out until the next day, so Trina spends the night in jail, and immediately after her release she bolts from her mother's car at a stoplight. At this point Trina's legal adulthood, although she is just a year out of high school, limits Keri's ability to aid and care for her daughter.

Having exhausted all of her possibilities, Keri finally decides to pursue conservatorship, which gives a parent the legal rights to commit an adult child to long-term hospitalization. Conservatorship is a long and difficult process, and Keri needs the advocacy of Trina's psychiatrist and a successful hearing that follows a temporary involuntary hospitalization in order to demonstrate the severity of Trina's condition. In this fictionalized account, we learn that being granted conservatorship requires a specific combination of circumstances: an initial hospitalization, an extension of the seventy-two-hour hold, a mental health court hearing before a judge, a psychiatric endorsement (which includes a fee for court appearance), an application with the Office of the Public Guardian, the selection of a locked facility in which to place the loved one, and paperwork to document each step of the process.

Despite the bureaucracy and the hurdles, when Trina is finally brought in for a hold Keri makes an attempt to gain conservatorship, but is unsuccessful because Trina's usual psychiatrist is out of town. Trina is released, and Keri must start the tedious process over again. She feels defeated, exhausted, and desperate as she continues to cope with her mentally ill daughter.

Campbell captures the weariness, discouragement, and helplessness that parents might feel as they attempt to navigate the mental health system and advocate for the care of their loved one. She clarifies the difference in care between county facilities and expensive private hospitals and the "red tape" that leaves parents in the middle of multiple service providers and stakeholders. For Trina's regular care, her "team" includes a psychiatrist, a psychologist, and her group program director. Keri is the "go-between," ensuring the continuity of care between all partners. When she attempts to gain conservatorship, she must also manage information sharing with hospital nurses, administrative assistants, and doctors at the county facility. At home, she has to build a relationship with the police and the System-wide Mental Assessment Response Team (SMART) so that they are aware of Trina's history when they respond to an emergency call. Although Keri is subject to communication gaps and issues that emerge with all the parties involved in Trina's care, she is considered "lucky." Her middle-class status affords her time, resources, and insurance coverage. But this luck runs short when Trina reaches the maximum days of hospitalization covered in one calendar year. Her class privilege only gets her so far as the insurance runs out and she is not eligible for free state or federal health benefits. At this point, Keri is at odds with a social worker who wants to release Trina from the hospital. Luckily, another health-system professional intervenes on their behalf, informing all parties that the discharge is actually against policy. Campbell demonstrates how difficult it can be to manage the mental health care system. Even for someone with education, class, or race privilege, the bureaucracy can be overwhelming. In addition, it can be far more challenging to negotiate for those with less privilege or none at all.

Trina's experience is only one account of the struggle with mental illness. Throughout the novel, Campbell clarifies that mental health issues also occur among the rich and the very poor. Keri remarks on seeing famous celebrities and "has beens" when she visits Trina during her holds at both the private hospital and at the county facility. Some parents in the novel have mentally ill adult children who are in jail, missing, or suffering with greater severity compared to Trina, and far more go undiagnosed and untreated. Campbell introduces minor story lines to comment on the class and race differences and the high incidence of undiagnosed mental illness in black communities. Early on in the novel, while Trina is stable and between episodes, we meet a character who is diminutively known as "Crazy Man." One afternoon, the mother and daughter head over to the commercial strip in their Crenshaw neighborhood to check out the vendors and floral markets. On their way they encounter a "neighbor" of sorts many readers can relate to:

Half a block away, Crazy Man was standing near one of the IP (incense people). Some of my neighbors referred to him that way, and even though I, of all people, should have known better, I did too. Mumbling to the air around him, he appeared to have schizophrenia but seemed harmless. According to some neighbors, he had been normal until he came back from Vietnam. Others swore his troubles began during high school. Crazy Man trekked in and around the community all day long, returning at night to his mother's house. His hair was a matted clump that hadn't seen shampoo, comb, brush, or scissors in a decade. He was clad in ancient dirty pants and a ragged shirt. His feet were bare and filthy. It would take heavy-duty equipment to get him clean. That and a crew. If mania and hallucinations, delusions, and paranoia have an odor, then that's what was rising out of his pores. Maybe pain, loss, and fury too.[8]

Campbell attempts to highlight the normalcy and prevalence of undiagnosed mentally ill persons in communities and the ease with which they are stigmatized as crazy. Her description of the disheveled homeless or wandering person is familiar, and even those who "should know better" see them with some level of disdain. This character also speaks to the impact of war and combat for the many veterans who suffer from post-traumatic stress disorder and other forms of mental illness. Crazy Man's description precedes a scene in which he steps out in front of her car into oncoming traffic, oblivious to any danger. Keri panics and slams on the brakes just in time. Later in the novel, that same day, she loses track of Trina in the floral market and finds her on the street talking to Crazy Man. At this juncture Crazy Man is also figurative and reflects Keri's fears, anxieties, and denial about Trina's illness. The implication is that she does not want her child either associated with or to be like Crazy Man. The novel parallels the reality that undiagnosed mental illness in African Americans can yield indefinite suffering and sometimes end tragically. Later, Keri grieves when she hears the news that Crazy Man was shot and killed by the police while having some sort of episode on Crenshaw Boulevard. Celestine, a minor character in the novel, signifies: "When somebody black get to acting a fool out in these streets, the cops gonna shoot 'em and go on about they business. Just like they killed that man over on Crenshaw."[9] Keri is alarmed and disturbed by this tragedy:

> I could taste fear in my mouth as I drove toward home. Maybe I began to grieve in my car, shedding tears for Crazy Man, crying hard, as if I knew him. Or maybe because I didn't want to know him. . . . It could have been Trina I thought. Those words bombarded me for the rest of the day. My child could have been the one being buried. She could have walked out of my house, bent on mayhem and destruction. There wasn't anything I could do to protect her.[10]

This moment also resonates with the occasional news stories about African American victims who are killed when police mistakenly perceived them as a threat. She is clearly speaking to the lack of awareness about mental illness within the criminal justice system. Such occurrences are not only a risk for poor, homeless, or vagrant people. Campbell poses this squarely as an issue of race and racial profiling by police, such that Keri even fears for Trina's safety within their middle-class residential enclave. In one instance, she has to call the police during a mental health emergency and is asked if Trina is armed or dangerous. Keri thinks:

> Hard question. Not so much answering but dealing with the implications: a black girl going crazy with a hammer in front of cops. Eula Love, I thought, conjuring up an image of the mentally ill black woman shot dead by the LAPD as she brandished a knife in her front yard. "No. No. No! She isn't armed. She doesn't have a weapon. She is a minor. Please, don't hurt her."[11]

The mother is clear that the criminalization of the mentally ill combined with criminalization of African Americans/minorities makes for a dangerous recipe. This commentary also reflects themes of mental illness and homelessness/vagrancy and the post-traumatic stress disorder of war veterans while painting a broader picture that goes beyond Trina's battle with bipolar disorder.

Campbell situates the main character amid multiple communities and relationships to temper the turbulence of caring for Trina. Keri's parent group meetings offer an avenue of support that keeps her head above water when caring for Trina threatens to drown her and wear her down completely. Commuting to West Los Angeles, the wealthy and predominantly white side of town, she attends a support group that meets at a local church. Campbell writes:

> The meeting was on the west side of town, land of high real estate, fair-skinned people, and the coldest ice. Part of me resented having to trek all the way from Crenshaw to get help for my child's issues. But the truth was, mental illness had a low priority on my side of the city, along with the color caste and the spread of HIV. Some things we just didn't talk about, even if it was killing us. So I had to come to the white people, who although just as traumatized, were a lot less stigmatized by whatever was wrong in their communities. All this is to say: It was easy to spot Gloria, Milton and Mattie in the crowd.[12]

Similar to Campbell's real life, Keri finds community with the handful of black parents in her support group. And much like the real life "NAMI mommies" who founded the NAMI Urban Los Angeles (NULA) chapter, this intimate circle of black parents offered mutual support, prayer, and the shared experience of black shame around mentally ill children. Keri and her friends, Gloria and Mattie, even fancied starting their own support group to provide resources in an African American community. After the support group meeting, they sometimes dined together, and the women expressed frustration about commuting across town and the absence of resources in their own neighborhoods. They talk about the stigma and denial that African Americans sometimes have about mental illness. At least two of the women reflected on ex-husbands who became absent fathers when their child was diagnosed with mental illness. Through these characters, Campbell suggests that the avoidance, shame, and loss that accompany mental illness are a heavy load to bear on top of the persistence of racism and disparity experienced by many African Americans.

Throughout the novel, Campbell revisits the shared pain of parents with mentally ill children, reaching across class lines from Keri's privileged middle-class position to Celestine, a poor working-class woman from Compton raising her grandchildren and trying to keep her thirty-something daughter on a straight path. Campbell also crosses the color line and connects Keri with a white support group member, Bethany, who is another single mom desperate to find long-term solutions for her daughter's care. This not only emphasizes the essential role of support and community but also the shared frustration with the bureaucracy and barriers to care within the current mental health system. The parents go beyond their lamentations and share strategies and tips for different aspects of mental health care. Similar to the prayer group that launched NULA in Campbell's real life, the parents' casual and formal support group discussions range from treatment, medication, and health insurance issues to self-care and pursuing conservatorship to helping an incarcerated loved one receive placement in the mental health section of a prison. Although Keri struggles with acceptance, together these parents recognize that their experiences are neither tragic nor insurmountable, but nonetheless life altering.

With the use of her novel Campbell is frame shifting[13] from the public campaign of NULA to the private sphere of the reader. As a work of fiction, *72 Hour Hold* extends the theoretical, instructional, and informational content about mental health awareness, issues, and resources provided by organizations like NULA. Together, these two vehicles, the public and the private, form a more effective campaign, reaching a broader constituency. Accordingly, and in the tradition of feminist thought, the personal and the political merge as the fictional literature reaches families and potential adherents within the privacy of their own homes. The novel works in complement to mental health activism and awareness campaigns by painting a lucid picture of the aspects of mental illness that are most difficult to understand and difficult to experience. Beyond the personal crises that families experience, Campbell highlights the stigma and silence around mental illness in black communities, as well as the shortcomings of the mental health system and the lack of resources. She addresses the dearth and the importance of community resources and support mechanisms for families of color. She also highlights the myriad of overarching social issues that inform mental health care (to include class, race, homelessness, the impact of war, and the criminalization of the mentally ill). She goes further and provides readers with tools to envision improved conditions and care for persons with mental illness. Amazingly, the narrative is skillfully crafted and does not read as preachy or propagandistic. Instead, *72 Hour Hold* works in concert with formal activism; Campbell uses the fictional story to connect readers and nurture understanding and compassion. Ultimately, *72 Hour Hold* uses lived experiences presented in fictional form to build a bridge to a cause in which Campbell was greatly invested.

While all of Campbell's novels (starting with *Your Blues Ain't Like Mine*) prioritize African American historical experience, her later novels experiment with different ways of infusing historical memory into contemporary fictional narratives. In her second and third novels she utilizes flashbacks, and in her fourth novel she combines flashback with a spirit presence that facilitates remembrance throughout the central plot. In *72 Hour Hold* Campbell continues to use personal recollection and a few flashbacks but also endeavors a new direction with the use of racial/epic memory.[14] Racial memory becomes the vehicle that Campbell uses to connect the traumatic experience of enslavement to the lived hardships of the present—in this case, coping with mental illness. For example, she uses metaphoric flashes to enslavement and the Underground Railroad, and direct references to Harriet Tubman[15] to represent brain disease as a form of "mental slavery." In one television interview Campbell notes, "Mental illness is a kind of slavery. We won't always have to hide and run and do our work in the dark. The day is coming when people with brain diseases won't be written off or warehoused, when everyone will know that recovery is possible."[16] Campbell goes a step further and uses this racial memory metaphor to transform hopelessness and despair into willful survival and faith. The characters in *72 Hour Hold* find a shared sense of suffering and unexpected community in other families and individuals coping with mental illness. This community is also extended to a kinship with enslaved African men and women of the past who risked and fought for their own lives and the lives of their children.

Keri is troubled by her own past as much as she is distraught by her daughter's diagnosis of bipolar disorder. Keri has flashes of emotion that connect her experience with mental illness to the Middle Passage, the auction block, the plantation, enslavement, escape, the Underground Railroad, and emancipation/manumission. The parallel between enslavement and mental illness ushers a deepened sense of historical remembrance that ultimately unshackles Keri's distress and despair. Thus Campbell facilitates a plausible healing and reconciliation for each novel's central conflict. Additionally, Campbell's literary use of remembrance also provides readers an intimate glance at African American life, history, and culture throughout different eras in the United States, illustrating the relevance of historical happenings to current lived experiences.

Keri's battles are first placed in historical context via metaphorical flashes to the maternal loss suffered by enslaved African women in the United States. She conjures the memory of the devastating forced migration of the Middle Passage experience that followed capture of African people prior to their enslavement in the Americas.[17] She then connects the dehumanizing objectification and separation associated with the auction block where African captives were sold off as chattel. After her daughter's first violent manic episode, Keri reflects:

> I embarked on my own Middle Passage that night, marching backward, ankles shackled. I journeyed to a Charleston auction block, screaming as my child was torn from my arms, as I watched her being driven away. Trina didn't belong to me anymore. Something more powerful possessed her. I saw her hand moving swiftly toward me, the fingers tightening into a ball, then opening again. The first blow was a slap, the next a punch.[18]

Trina's violent episode is likened to the Middle Passage, such that this event is traumatic and marked the beginning of the long journey ahead. Keri despairs the initial ordeal as involuntary bondage for her and her daughter. The auction block extends the Middle Passage metaphor as she sees the mental health episode as something that has separated her from her daughter and abruptly uprooted the normalcy and stability of their family. Similarly, on a real auction block family members would be sold away, separated, and relocated to an unfamiliar place with conditions that were equally harsh or sometimes worse. For Trina and Keri, the diagnosis of mental illness is marked by separation and loss. Keri's distress is so devastating that remembrance in the context of the Middle Passage and the auction block become the only way for her to make meaning of this experience.

As Keri watches her child driven away in a police car, an officer tries to console her with the "affirmation" that she can endure because she "is a strong woman." Here Campbell inserts: "Strong enough to plant a crop, pick cotton, birth a baby in the field, and keep on working."[19] This conjures imagery found at the source of the narrow archetype of the enduring, long-suffering "strong black woman" rooted in the enslaved African woman's hardship.[20] This perception of black women and black mothers, on the plantation and contemporarily, both marginalizes and diminishes the physical and emotional pain endured, not to mention the importance of respite and assistance in black women's lives. Black women on the plantation often performed grueling labor, sometimes while pregnant, nursing, and caring for children (along with suffering from sexual assault, which was commonplace for enslaved women and girls). Likewise, Keri's burden as a divorced mother without assistance at home requires profound emotional labor that invokes the physical labor expected of her enslaved foremothers. Keri watches her daughter's repeated episodes of mania, in fear that the late night routine would, once again, escalate to provocative clothing, gaudy makeup, and Trina heading to the streets into danger. The mother's worry leaves her "mesmerized and terrorized, like a whip dangling from ol' massa's hand."[21] Keri's fear of the "whip" and the subsequent "violent beating" that follows both connects her to the past and also clarifies the intensity and anguish experienced by families with mental illness. The whip and the beating signify Trina's unstable behavior, which is not only impulsive but dangerous to herself and to others. Keri imagines the plight of her foremothers on the plantation who were likewise faced with unreasonable, unyielding, and painful expectations of endurance and self-sacrifice. Likening herself to enslaved women helps her to process societal expectations about her maternal responsibility as well as her sense of helplessness.

Campbell continues with well-placed insertions of epic memory as Keri's journey waxes and wanes as Trina struggles with her illness. Later, Keri equates her daughter's period of stability, which follows three climactic hospitalizations, with "receiving grace from a sympathetic 'massa' granting manumission to both mother and child."[22] Similarly, after an extended hospitalization, Trina returns home calm and compliant with her counseling and meds, and Keri thinks: a reprieve. Massa had changed his mind, brought back the slave child, and placed her in her mother's arms along with manumission papers for both.[23] The concept of manumission and reprieve evokes the master-slave narrative that Keri has embraced to cope with her caregiver experience and the sense of victimhood and vulnerability she feels. Trina's mental illness has "indentured" her mother into a servitude that is marked by distress and desperation. Ultimately, Keri is likened to the mothers on the plantation, who amid horrible suffering desire the safety and proximity of their children above all.

This use of racial memory takes interesting twists and turns throughout 72 Hour Hold with a dynamic parallel to the Underground Railroad. When Trina runs away and sends an angry email to Keri threatening suicide, her mother feels a sense of helplessness and exhaustion and seeks ancestral support: "What would Harriet do with this? No time to plan. Nowhere to run. But the same imperative, the same need to cross the border. To save herself. Then save another."[24] As the plot of the novel develops, Keri and Trina go "underground" in pursuit of a radical, illegal treatment program to stabilize Trina once and for all. Having "kidnapped" her own daughter, Keri calls on inspiration from the ancestors once again as she takes flight. She relates to the song lyrics "Steal Away to Jesus" from an early spiritual that was used to provide coded messages for the Underground Railroad:

> Steal away, steal away, steal away home. I ain't got long to stay here. Gabriel Prosser. Denmark Vesey. Nat Turner. Harriet Tubman. Did they all begin with secret meetings and whispered plans? Did they change their minds more than once? To steal away home was more than a notion.[25]

By far, the majority of Campbell's references to historical memory in 72 Hour Hold center on the Underground Railroad. In one interview she remarks on her admiration of Harriet Tubman, who is also referenced multiple times in the novel. The Underground Railroad parallel foreshadows the metaphorical escape and the risks associated with shifting from the "shame and victimhood" paradigm that Keri has embraced in response to familial mental illness.

In relation to mental illness, the escape narrative is central to Keri, who never seems to accept or adjust to Trina's diagnosis and the ups and downs that she comes to think of as "the devastation." Her emotional pain is so intense that she must conjure up one of the most harrowing experiences in African American history in order to find understanding, kinship, and hope. And while Keri initially focuses on the suffering and the horror of her experience, she eventually draws from the shared pain of American slavery and mental illness, a sort of inspiration that parallels the historical narrative of freedom and emancipation. By the novel's end Keri has learned to manage her transformed life and begins the path of acceptance and healing that liberates her from the weight of mental slavery that affects her and her daughter. Overall, the use of the epic memory, or "collective" unconscious, to weave historical reference into the text is a new and innovative departure from Campbell's usual strategy of transgenerational plot lines and flashbacks. Simultaneously, this convention of historical remembrance contextualizes the sociopolitical commentary that aligns with her personal commitment to mental health activism. Campbell's enslavement metaphor connects mental illness with African American historical memory in order to build compassion around two painful and traumatic experiences. In doing so, she amplifies the frame of concern to inspire readers to become meaningfully invested in the cause of mental health awareness. The practice of frame amplification expands from providing information to helping people make the connections that lead to involvement in a social cause.

In *72 Hour Hold* the analysis of black women's racialized gender experience centers primarily on the issue of motherhood. While it is clear, and important to note, that motherhood and black womanhood are not synonymous, it is also true that motherhood is a distinctly female experience that is significant for many women. Black motherhood is also an important site for examining the intersections of racism, sexism, and classism.[26] Keri suffers and lives in secret after her daughter is diagnosed with mental illness. Similar to Delotha in *Your Blues*, Keri struggles with feeling like a bad mother and also deals with maternal loss on several levels. Furthermore, her troubled relationship with her own mother worsens things. The isolation that she creates by avoiding old friends, keeping the diagnosis a secret, and managing Trina's care alone leads to multiple issues for Keri. In her solitude, she regularly questions her parenting, struggles with jealousy, and compares her situation to parents with healthy young adult children. She grieves for the aspirations and hopes she had of Trina attending college, living independently, and being successful. She soothes herself by comparing Trina to young adults with more severe brain disease issues. The heavy stigma of mental illness leaves Keri longing for a normalcy that is unlikely and inconsistent with her daughter's diagnosis. Thus she continually grapples with guilt, self-doubt, shame, and grief. Her motherhood experiences are further complicated because she is a divorced single mother without the support that she desires and because her own mother abandoned her in a struggle with alcoholism.

Historically, black mothers have been cast in a negative light—from the emasculating matriarchs described in the infamous Moynihan report[27] to the later image of the Welfare Queen.[28] Patricia Hill Collins identifies these stereotypes as "controlling images" that impact black women and how they are perceived by society. Within mainstream media, *Claudine*, a popular 1974 film, attempts to rouse and critique the Welfare Queen stereotype as well. Starring Diahnn Carroll as a single mother of six, the film depicts her struggle with poverty and the bureaucracy of the welfare system that denies her support if she attempts to marry or hold a part-time job. In *72 Hour Hold* Keri is haunted by the negative depictions of poor black mothers as unfit. Her shame also dates back to enslavement when black women could neither nurture their own children nor protect them from beatings, rape, or being sold away.[29] Keri embodies this experience with disgrace and doubt about the quality of her motherhood. She takes Trina's diagnosis with bipolar disorder personally, assuming and imagining that it is a direct result of bad parenting. Thus, for her, it is proof that she is another "bad black mother":

> Ha! Isn't it always Mommy's fault? Mom didn't do this, she didn't do that. She nursed too long; she bottle-fed. She slapped the shit out of the kid; she raised a spoiled brat. She was too dumb and lazy to get a job; she worked full-time and never paid attention. She weighed 300 pounds and waddled into school for open house; she weighed 110 and

showed too much cleavage. She got high; she was too uptight. She traded Dad in for a lesbian lover; she did everything her man told her to do. She stayed with a husband who beat her and set a poor example; she left the fool and broke up the family or, worse yet, she kicked his ass and started running things. She let her boyfriends spend the night; she didn't provide a male role model. She never cleaned; she screamed when the little ones tracked in mud. Lazy cow fed the kids McDonald's every night. Negligent slob didn't attend the PTA. Too trifling to help sell Girl Scout cookies. She let her child run wild and had herself a good ol' time. Her child was drowning, and she didn't save her.[30]

Here we see that Campbell takes on the "controlling images" of black womanhood by using Keri's internalized anxiety to expose the microscope and the unflinching judgment placed on black mothers. Keri's distress suggests there is a "no-win" situation in which mothers will be frowned upon for any and every shortcoming or action that may or may not impact their children. Even though such expectations are unreasonable, Keri is correct about the likelihood that she will be judged and that her daughter's actions will be read as a direct reflection of her worth and parental ability. This is evident when a seventy-year-old neighbor, Mrs. Winslow, comforts Keri after observing Trina's mania while her mother was away from the house. As the older woman comforts Keri, she embraces her and rubs her back while she launches a major insult:

"You younger women had all those options. Walked out on your husbands because you wanted to be so much. I heard about your store. Might have worked out better if you'd stayed home and raised your kids." She spoke evenly, never stopped rubbing my back, and gave me an odd, surprised look when I pulled away. Mrs. Winslow stood in my entryway for a while before she finally closed the door behind her.[31]

In effect, Mrs. Winslow, in arrogance and ignorance about mental illness, has judged Keri as a "bad black mother." While this offends Keri, it is consistent with her feelings of shame and guilt about Trina. Furthermore, such instances fuel Keri's compulsion to conceal Trina's condition and her own suffering. Campbell situates this character to illustrate the intersection of black maternal guilt with the doubt, shame, and self-criticism that accompanies parenting a mentally ill child. This juncture would recur for Keri throughout the novel.

Along with shame and stigma, Keri experiences a lot of unresolved hurt and resentment. As she imagines concealing the situation in which Trina hits her, she also recalls other pains and wounds that she has kept secret and holds on to her feelings of guilt:

> The assault was meant to be a secret that got locked up in the internal vault, along with Uncle-Danny-liked-to-play-peepee-games-with-me or Mommy-used-to-get-drunk-every-night-and-that's-how-come-I-stay-with-Ma-Missy. Your pedophile uncle and your alkie mama aren't your fault, however. Your child, however, is always your fault. If she grows up to be president you did a good job. If he wears a black trench coat and starts shooting up the place with his buddies, well I'm damn sure I didn't want to see that particular judgment reflected in anybody's eyes.[32]

Here we see that Keri possesses an intricate web of childhood and adult trauma that emerges as she tries to cope with her own daughter. The resentment begins with her own mother who suffered with alcoholism during Keri's childhood. Although she was raised by her loving grandmother, Keri grieves her childhood and longs for a healthy, attentive mother. She cleaves to the negative memories and the trauma of witnessing her mother coming home drunk, passing out, or arguing with her grandmother outside in front of neighbors and schoolmates. Keri remembers her mother missing Parent Night because she was passed out. She tries futilely to rouse her and begins crying in her grandmother's embrace. Ma Missy tells her:

> "Be grateful, baby. One of these days she'll be all right, and you won't even remember the bad times. Plenty things worse than a drunk mama. Be strong girl." But I had never learned to be grateful for having less than I really wanted.[33]

Thus Keri's motherhood experience is haunted by the trauma of being the daughter of an alcoholic. Keri's hurt remains with her into adulthood as her mother, now sober and recovering, tries to repair their relationship. Keri refuses Emma's calls and her attempts to reconcile. She shies away from the similarities between Emma's alcoholism and Trina's mental illness and keeps the diagnosis from her mother altogether. Also, as a divorced single mother, Keri effectively rejects a potential avenue of familial support and continues to cope with Trina alone. Campbell appears to relate Keri's negative mother-daughter relationship with Emma to the fear of failing her own child, Trina.

Keri's failed marriage is another factor that breeds resentment and also impacts her motherhood experience. Her ex-husband, Clyde, leaves his wife and daughter early in the marriage (during Trina's adolescence) in pursuit of his ambitious career goals. Clyde becomes a "paycheck" dad providing financial support in place of quality time. He struggles to accept Trina's diagnosis and criticizes Keri for forcing medication and mental health care on their teenage daughter. He believes that Trina is just going through "a tough time" typical of teenagers. Keri tries to explain to Clyde:

> "It's more than that. Something is seriously wrong with Trina." He shook his head. "It's just a stage," he said. No amount of arguing could persuade my ex-husband that whatever was going on with Trina wasn't a part of normal adolescence. But his logic didn't sway me. After he left, I called the police. When Trina finally returned home, they were waiting. They heard her hysterical threats at the door. I followed their car as they drove to the hospital. When I called Clyde from the psychiatric ward, he yelled at me that I was overreacting. "I won't have anything to do with this!" he said, and then he hung up.[34]

But his denial leaves Keri feeling isolated and solely responsible for the care and burden of a mentally ill child. For much of the novel he dismisses Trina's mental illness as "obviously some mother-daughter stuff"[35] arising as Trina prepares to leave for college. Beyond the current experience with Clyde, we also learn, through flashback, that the couple lost an infant son to crib death in the early years of their marriage. The two of them avoided grieving openly or supporting one another as they processed this devastating lost. They are once again alienated from one another as they come to grips with Trina's illness. When Trina is hospitalized again and calls her father to the hospital, Keri arrives and sees him at the sign-in desk:

"Clyde."

"Trina called me last night and told me she was here. What happened, Keri?"

"She was at her program, and she started becoming manic."

"Why didn't you call me?"

"I . . ."

"I'm her father. I have a right to know. There was no reason to have her put in a psychiatric hospital."

My voice began to rise. "She hit somebody. And for the record, I didn't have her put in the hospital. The group leader did. But I agree with her."

"So what if she hit someone? Maybe the person deserved it. Maybe he did something to her. I'm getting her out of here."

"Clyde, Trina was smoking marijuana. That may have been what triggered this episode."

"She doesn't belong here."

"It's only for three days. They'll get her back on her medication. That's what's essential. You don't understand."

"I'm signing her out." Clyde said, staring at me.

"You can't do that, Clyde. Nobody can. She's on a three-day involuntary hold. The law says she has to stay here."

"Damn!" His frustration was etched into the lines across his forehead.

I put my hand on his arm, mostly to calm myself. "Let's just go see her."

He pulled away from me. "You go first."[36]

This passage reveals the tension between Trina's parents and the emotional distance between them in times of hardship. Whereas Collins highlights the role and value of community support and "othermothers" who share the responsibility, Keri is without part-ner support or assistance from other avenues.[37] It is clear that this isolation brings her close to a breaking point, fueling her despera-tion and angst.

Campbell reveals these issues through Keri's motherhood experience and foreshadows a necessary shift and steps for recon-ciliation for Keri, beginning with the need to forgive her mother and her ex-husband, Clyde, for her feelings of abandonment. It becomes evident that Keri's immediate motherhood experience is informed by her own childhood trauma, feelings of rejection and abandonment from a failed marriage, and the guilt and grief over the death of her infant son years earlier. This is a far more vex-ing position from which to care for Trina and her mental illness. Accordingly, Keri is a time bomb. Without meaningful emotional work, she is unable to care for herself or for Trina. She must ulti-mately reconcile her self-perception as a woman and as a mother and also address the need for support and assistance. While Keri does not fall into the stereotype and is not a bad parent, she must address her self-care and emotional work to better assist her daughter. This work begins with the generational wounds with her mother, Emma, and continues with seeking and accepting support from others. By extending the frame to include racialized gender issues in the conversation about mental illness and coping, Camp-bell adds new concerns that are relevant to readers. Keri's moth-erhood experience introduces issues that can affect how families deal with the mental illness of a loved one. Accordingly, Campbell's act of frame extension brings attention to the personal wounds and emotions that arise when families begin to address a loved one's mental illness. In Keri's case, and in the support groups that Campbell led within the NULA affiliate, having a family member with mental illness can bring to the surface unrelated problems and traumas. Keri learns that her own issues and hurts must also be addressed to effectively care for a mental health consumer and to ensure the overall mental health and wellness of her family.

In 72 *Hour Hold* Campbell continues to resolve her plotlines with themes of healing and reconciliation. As identified in the close reading of *Your Blues Ain't Like Mine* (chapter 3), her resolutions are less about neat happy endings and more about the human spirit and the relationships of her protagonists. Whereas *Your Blues* endeavors to redeem many of the novel's deeply flawed characters, *72 Hour Hold* provides reconciliation of Keri's wounds, such that she eventually accepts and healthily manages extremely difficult life circumstances. In both instances, Campbell offers new beginnings as a window of hope through which characters can begin to heal the wounds and problems depicted in the novel. In *72 Hour Hold* Keri is the primary vehicle for recurring themes of healing, forgiveness, and reconciliation. In addition to the very real and present distress and feelings of loss over her daughter's turbulent battle with mental illness, Keri has several emotional injures that aggravate and impede her ability to cope with and accept Trina's illness. These hurts begin with her estrangement from her own mother, a recovering alcoholic who was unstable and volatile throughout her childhood. As an adult, she harbors emotions from her divorce from her ex-husband—Trina's father—and the devastating loss of her newborn son to crib death early in their marriage. Overall, Keri's feelings of emotional abandonment are deeply entrenched.

As the novel climaxes, Keri's healing process is triggered by a complex sequence of events. When her first pursuit of conservatorship falls through after Trina's third seventy-two-hour hospitalization, Keri fearfully anticipates her daughter's release from the hospital with distress and frustration. With Bethany's persuasion, she opts for an illegal underground treatment option, simply known as the "Program," rather than starting over, trusting the mental health system, and attending support group. She reflects on her desperation:

> Later when I'd try to remember what propelled me over the edge, I could never say with any degree of certainty what final wind blew me there. All I knew was, my child would never be able to say I didn't try hard enough. A click went off in my mind, and I was racing across the plantation in the dark.[38]

Again we see that Keri is acting out her own guilt and compulsion to "save" her daughter. She is unable to surrender control and take steps toward acceptance. When Keri and Trina depart with Bethany; her daughter, Angelica; and the program leader, Brad, she has no idea of their destination or what to expect. Brad takes the wallets and identification from each mother to prevent the daughters from stealing them and attempting to leave. Keri is put off, but yields with uncertainty: "I was the runaway, hidden in the back of the wagon under the hay. That was me, holding my breath, saying my prayers, trying to make it to a safe haven."[39] Once again Keri relies on ancestral memory, this time from the Underground Railroad, to understand and frame her experience. She proceeds with uncertainty as Trina and Angelica are transported to remote locations and hosted by parents of former Program participants. The girls begin a routine of regimented nutrition, exercise, and recreational and work activities, and they are also administered moderated doses of medication. During the first stop, the facilitator, Brad, challenges Keri to accept Trina's mental illness:

> "You're like a lot of parents. You think your daughter's bipolar disorder is your personal tragedy, but it's not. It's Trina's. She is the one with the brain disease, not you. You want the bright child back, who attends Brown and gets straight A's. Well don't we all. You have to accept Trina the way she is. She's not something you ordered from a catalog. She's a gift from God. You need to treat her that way."
>
> "I love my child."
>
> He puts his hands on my wrist. "I'm not talking about love. I'm talking about reverence for her life."
>
> Brad squeezed my wrist and then let it go.
>
> When I looked at Brad and Jan, I realized they wanted me to surrender my dreams of Trina's complete recovery. Maybe that was another reason to leave.[40]

Keri is being asked to take a very difficult step in surrendering dreams and hopes she held for her teenage daughter; she remains reluctant and doubtful.

Keri's disinclination to surrender control is evident in several instances throughout the novel. Repeatedly, loved ones and other parents with mentally ill children warn Keri not to give her life away to the illness. It takes some time for her to understand this, but the following exchanges foretell the shift that is to come. Ultimately, she must move from victimhood to responsibility in a difficult situation. Talking to another parent (of a woman who had run off with Trina early in the novel), Keri is advised:

> "Don't stress yourself out," Celestine said as I was leaving. "Melody get here when she get her. Same with your girl. Social worker told me you gotta pace yourself, otherwise you end up getting broke down. Right before Melody got into that program, my pressure shot up so high the doctor was talking about putting me in the hospital. I gotta take care of me, Yeah." Celestine sounded as though she'd been to group.[41]

Later, when Trina is released from a "hold" and promises to take her meds responsibly, a trusted coworker offers:

> "It's not going to be that easy," Frances told me a few days later, when I was rhapsodizing about Trina's progress, the resumption of her old life, our old life. But I dismissed her caution. I had set my sights on the Promised Land, and that was the only place I wanted to live.[42]

While traveling between sites of the underground treatment program Keri looks at Bethany's daughter, Angelica, with eyes of judgment because she is "worse off" than Trina. Angelica has schizoaffective disorder (which is a combination of multiple mental illness traits), self-medicates by cutting (self-mutilation), and is addicted to "meth" (crystal methamphetamine). It is also implied that Angelica has sex for drugs. Keri apologizes to the other mother for hurting her feelings, but Bethany reacts strongly, attacking Keri's denial and self-righteousness:

> "My feelings? F--- my feelings. Don't you dare write my kid off. . . . I'm not here because I want her to get a degree from Brown and meet the perfect young man. I want to keep her alive. That may not be enough for you, but it's enough for me. . . . You should try to see the God in her."[43]

Keri tries to calm her friend: "'All right, I hear you.' . . . But really, I didn't."[44] Keri holds fast to her unwillingness to rethink her perception of and response to Trina's mental illness, and her unyielding desire to "fix" Trina and restore normalcy to their lives.

Midway through the Program, Keri speaks to another parent about their shared experiences. She has grown weary after Trina attempts to jump out of the car on the way to their next destination. At the second site, a rural farm property, she meets the owners, Pete and his wife, Cecilia, who has suffered from a stroke. Drawing from her early career as a massage therapist, Keri lends the woman her gift of touch. She soothes Cecilia, who uses a wheelchair, with light massage as she enjoys the afternoon sitting under a tree. Pete talks about the long-term struggle with their own mentally ill daughter and his support of the Program and what they are trying to do, despite having only moderate success stabilizing his own daughter. The older man speaks to Keri of the impact of the stress and self-neglect on each parent's physical health and loosely associates Cecilia's stroke with her inability to let go of their daughter: "When you love someone who has mental illness, there comes a point at which you must detach in order to preserve your own life. My wife couldn't do that."[45] Pete, who is a doctor, explains his theory further to clarify:

> "It was her reaction that made her sick. We all have the potential for pathology in our bodies. Cells can react negatively at any given time. Stress can set those cells in motion on a journey to self-destruction. Each one of us is responsible for defending our own bodies from that kind of assault. My wife wouldn't rest. She wouldn't eat well. She wouldn't guard her emotions."[46]

He also talks about the usefulness of the mental health system once you learn how to navigate it, but concludes that patients' rights ultimately limit a parent's influence and often the pursuit of necessary care: "Once we got the right information, I must say that the system worked very well for us, up to a point; patients' rights. Patients' rights often clash with what's best for a mentally-ill person."[47] Pete offers several gems of wisdom to Keri about his twenty-year journey through mourning, acceptance, and settling into a peaceful life on their farm:

> "Growing things provided me with a simple seasonal routine. It's a good routine for someone who is in mourning. You can't always beat what is difficult in your life. Sometimes you have to let it win and shout hallelujah anyhow."[48]

As he departs, he asks Keri to massage his ailing wife later. Keri is intrigued by Pete and his viewpoint, but in her own mind rejects his ideas about acceptance and releasing control. She thinks to herself:

> I'd treat his wife, but I'd never agree with him. I hadn't brought Trina on this journey to accept the cards I'd been dealt. I was here to throw in that hand and pick up the one I was supposed to have.[49]

This final instance of rejecting the insight of other people who share her experience would precede circumstances that place Keri squarely in the face of her fears and worries and on the road toward acceptance and healing. Despite her stubbornness to shift her thinking, the seeds have been planted for Keri to sow and nurture when she is ready to do so.

Keri and Trina's experience with the Program goes terribly wrong, in part because of Keri's resistance but also because of Trina's second and successful attempt to run away after arriving at their third stop on the way to the final destination. This time they are in an urban area, but Keri is unsure of her exact whereabouts because of Brad's security measures. The adults search local hangouts and drug spots, but to no avail. With Trina being missing overnight, Keri is beside herself. By morning she receives a call from her ex-husband, Clyde, informing her that Trina has been detained at the local mental health hospital, near Sacramento. Separately, Clyde and Keri's ex-boyfriend, Orlando, drive over seven hours from Los Angeles to support Keri, and she grapples internally with confusion about her relationships with the two men. This sequence of events ushers a breaking point that forces Keri toward the healing that she has resisted thus far.

Clyde's arrival provides multiple opportunities for Keri to reconcile her feelings of rejection and abandonment. A weary argument, followed by several heartfelt conversations, allows Keri to express her hurt and usher Clyde out of denial to an open and vulnerable position. Clyde is reluctant but realizes that Keri has exhausted several avenues of care and has been attentive and thorough with Trina's situation. He attends a support group meeting while waiting to visit with Trina and cries for the first time, for both Trina and the child he and Keri lost many years ago. He apologizes to Keri but also points out her penchant for holding grudges. Keri must squarely examine her issues of forgiveness. While waiting in Sacramento, Keri and Clyde are able to have more heartfelt conversations about Trina. When Trina is released for transfer to a local hospital back in Los Angeles, both parents ride together to transport their daughter, and the tension of the past begins to ease for Keri. Their honesty and clarity about Trina's mental illness traverse the huge valley between them so that they can move forward with less baggage and begin cooperating on Trina's mental health care. Clyde eventually supports Keri's pursuit of conservatorship and full financial support of his daughter's care, but he still struggles with offering a consistent presence to Trina. Keri finally begins to find peace, accepting that Clyde's shortcomings are not malicious or personal when she recognizes that his flaws appear in his two subsequent marriages. She realizes that although she longed for him to co-parent Trina with her, she neither loves him nor desires his partnership. This helps her to move forward and be more open in her relationship with Orlando.

When Keri returns home to Los Angeles from the Program, she is able to finally gain conservatorship of Trina. Trina is enrolled in a ninety-day program at a locked facility that both parents agree is safe and professional. At home and alone, Keri ponders all that has happened, ultimately acknowledging that

> Trina was going to be in and out of sanity for the rest of her life and
> I'd just have to deal with that. Ma Missy had learned that lesson a long
> time ago. Why couldn't I? Why did I keep holding out for rescues and

miracles and perfect endings? The program had tried to disabuse me of that notion. Jean and Eddie, Pete and Cecilia, Margaret—even Celestine, Melody's mother frying hamburgers for three grandchildren and holding her breath until her daughter made it home at night—*they'd all learned acceptance.* Things could be worse. Much worse.[50] (italics mine)

Finally taking the first step, recognizing the need for acceptance, she begins to rally her resources. Keri experiences more relief than defeat after returning to the support group and getting assistance on how to navigate the system and the possibility of having to start over from scratch to stabilize Trina. She also begins to accept phone calls from her mother, Emma, and the two begin to talk daily, after a difficult start. Keri must finally stop avoiding when her mother shows up to press forth the healing and to help Keri out at the boutique. When Emma shows up unexpectedly, Keri agrees to accept her help, and the healing begins:

My mother's eyes met mine. We'd escaped from a terrible land, thrown off our shackles, and crossed borders. What we acknowledged to each other in that swift, silent glance was that from now on it was all about and only about time—maddening, exhilarating time—passing, doing its job, setting us free.[51]

With time and willingness as essential tools, Keri has decidedly taken steps toward forgiveness and healing. Furthermore, the reconciliation with Clyde and Emma allows for new avenues of support for Keri and Trina. It also opens Keri emotionally to move forward with her boyfriend, Orlando, and his teenage sons, as well as close friends whom she'd avoided since Trina's illness. Orlando moves in with Keri and functions as a loving, reliable partner willing to assist with Trina. These healing moments provide the tools Keri needs for accepting and living with Trina's illness. Releasing her resentment also leads to more supportive relationships that help her to share the care for Trina rather than doing it alone.

At the close of the novel, Trina is stabilized after she returns home from the ninety-day residential program. After a few difficult weeks, she adjusts to being home, and Keri finds a new psychiatrist to adjust Trina's medication and gradually lower her dosage. Orlando and Emma are now staying at the house, and Orlando's son, PJ, spends a lot of time there as well. Trina is pleased by the new familial arrangement at the house and even has a heart-to-heart with her grandmother about recovery and commitment to wellness. In addition to the loving social interaction in the house, Trina finds outlets for positive energy and self-expression. When Keri and her friends, Mattie and Gloria, begin a support group branch in their African American neighborhood near Crenshaw Avenue, Trina participates in the support group for consumers. The latter group engages in activity-based support and therapy, including the writing and performing of plays. Trina experiences success and creative expression through scriptwriting and acting in her own play at the local church where the groups meet. Both mother and daughter find meaningful work amid the daily presence of mental illness. The formation of Keri and Trina's support community is directly reminiscent of the women who joined Campbell to form NULA.

To begin to accept and reconcile the difficult reality of mental illness, Keri must heal and release old hurts. She ultimately has to approach freedom with new and realistic expectations, while creating new modes of stability, health, and balance within her family. On the one hand, she finds the need to release control; however, she also draws from the spiritual memory of African ancestors and their hope and determination. She identifies her strength as a black woman in ways that are not stereotypical. To fully embrace a new paradigm of freedom, remembrance, and ancestral connection, Keri must venture beyond the archetype or controlling image of the strong, enduring black woman and take steps toward self-care and reconciliation in her relationships. For Keri, remembrance helps her develop determination, wisdom, and increased faith as she takes these steps and as she manages her daughter's illness and instability. The symbolic remembrance also cultivates the healing of old wounds and losses that inhibited her ability to seek intimacy and support as she dealt with the difficulties of parenting an adult child with bipolar disorder. Thus the lessons embedded in the historical narrative of enslaved African women hold personal restorative value for the individual and her community.

When Keri reconnects with her friend Bethany, the two women reflect on their daughters' current period of stability, and Bethany remarks, "Honey . . . this is what they call a breather."[52] Keri places this concept of a "breather" (an opportunity to rest and restore following and or preceding a period of intense work) in the context of her personal and cultural history. In this final passage of the novel, Keri reflects:

> Long ago I sat on the top step with Ma Missy, watching my mother pass out on the living room floor from too much scotch. It was a bad time. Ma Missy held me close and I wriggled and writhed. She rocked me and hummed something that made me still, made me smile. Our song.
>
> Maybe after the devastation, what you're supposed to do is rebuild the space in your mind that's been blown away, but never fool yourself into thinking that it's stronger, that you've erected some impenetrable force that won't be hit again and again and again. Things fall down, people too. Crazy men wander the land, crashing and crumbling, and nobody gets a warning. There is always another swamp to cross. Passengers are both lost and found. Ol' Harriet learned that the hard way, the first time she retraced her path, erased her scent, outwitted the dogs, and followed the only star that lit the way, only to discover that when she got where she was going, new hounds were waiting. But there was that cool space on the bank of the murky water where she lay on fragrant moss, undisturbed for hours, and there was no barking, no sound of twigs snapping. A breather.[53]

Ultimately, Keri is able to create family routine and stability for Trina with the knowledge that hospitalization is always a possibility and that periods of calm and compliance could be followed by upheaval and a return to manic episodes. She enjoys the "breathers" and shares her life and her care of Trina with her mother; Orlando and his children; her ex-husband, Clyde; and old friends that she had previously avoided and cut off. Participation in activities gives meaning and value to Trina. Keri takes lessons from

Brad, Pete, and the other people whose advice she had ignored along the way. She cultivates meaning in her own life with many relationships, meaningful work, and emotional release of old hurts, disappointment, and guilt about Trina's mental illness. She finds her freedom in endeavoring to live her life fully and managing obstacles and hardships with a loving support system. Thus she is no longer "enslaved" by Trina's mental illness. Entering into this new freedom and acceptance, Keri and Trina must now rely on community, must compromise, and must work step-by-step through recovery, living their lives at a new pace and cadence. While Campbell uses the enslavement/emancipation metaphor for mental illness, she also foreshadows Keri's denial and reluctance to accept the difficulty of Trina's mental illness. Initially, Keri narrowly defined her freedom in terms of her past experiences of normalcy. By the end of the novel, Campbell provides Keri with a shift from the master-slave narrative to the freedom-hope narrative. Campbell asserts in one interview:

> The novel is a journey of sorts, . . . as I have had a journey. And the point of that journey is to bring you to acceptance. Life is *not* going to be the same. The way it was before their loved one began to manifest the symptoms of a mental illness. But can you adjust to this? Can you still feel joy? Can your loved one still be a productive one with friendships and love? Very, very possibly.[54]

The message is that a parent, family member, or caretaker of a person with mental illness can begin to envision a life with balance and support rather than isolation, despair, and suffering.

In *72 Hour Hold* Campbell writes about healing and reconciliation with intentionality and precision. Her convictions about acceptance ring through and reflect her own lived experience as a mental health activist and an African American mother whose daughter has mental illness. She highlights the importance of forgiveness on the journey toward healing and suggests the need to release hurts and resentments. By doing so, we see her main character, Keri, move from being controlling, distressed, and exhausted to being a woman with hope, faith, endurance, and a loving community. Previously, she was inclined to isolate herself and Trina, keeping the most intimate pain and vulnerability to herself. While her support group friends and many others were always present to provide assistance, information, and emotional support, Keri's transformation and healing positioned her to recognize and receive help and resources on her own accord. Additionally, the frequent mention of Keri's former career as a massage therapist and scenes in which she soothes Trina, friends, and strangers with her healing hands suggests the importance of touch, intimacy, and physical wellness (in the novel, many of the mothers of adult children with mental illness suffer minor to severe ailments). It also suggests that, for Keri, using one's gift, talent, or art can be healing in and of itself. One could also conclude this to be the case for Campbell as she transformed her activist work with NULA into a creative work of fiction written with healing and reconciliation in mind.

Campbell's theme of healing and reconciliation completes the final stage of the framing process, *frame transformation*. The writer transforms or shifts the way mental illness and mental health activism are viewed. She enacts a spiritual process for Keri to heal the emotional trauma that many parents like her struggle with. This suggests that, beyond education, support services, and policy changes, there is a deeper, internal work that is necessary. This is a difficult conceptual shift that nonetheless works in concert with activist efforts but also requires active steps and personal responsibility for individuals and families. Ultimately, it is a challenge much like the one posed in the culmination of her first novel, which centers on personal agency, relationship work, and reimagining a painful and tragic experience as something altogether new, hopeful, and promising.

The signature themes of Campbell's novel—historical memory, racial commentary, black women's racialized gender experience, and healing and forgiveness—recur clearly in her final novel, but take on distinct form within the discourse of mental health and awareness in African American communities. *72 Hour Hold* effectively informs, engages, and entertains but also offers tools for the most intimate challenges and experiences. It directly complements and extends the work she endeavored with the National Alliance on Mental Illness (NAMI), drawing in readers, families, and consumers into a discourse about the very personal life experiences facing millions of Americans.

*72 Hour Hold* offers a raw, vulnerable, and personal depiction of mental illness and its impact on a family. As the novel climaxes, Keri and Trina go "underground" to participate in a radical and illegal treatment program with hopes that it will stabilize and empower Trina in ways that the mental hospitals fail to do. Throughout the plot, Keri grapples with doubting her motherhood. As a result, several old wounds emerge to reveal multiple areas of healing that conflate the issue of Trina's illness. These struggles impede Keri's acceptance that her life and her daughter's life are forever changed. As a mother, Keri must surrender the hope that Trina's life will be anything like she has imagined it. The novel utilizes a parallel narrative that brings forth the traumatic experience of enslavement as a lens for contextualizing this black woman's suffering, pain, and healing amid her daughter's mental illness. In the end, Keri must accept Trina's illness and forgive her ex-husband, Clyde, and her mother, Emma.

While Campbell highlights the distinctive experience of an African American mother, many aspects of the fictional account transcend race, class, and gender boundaries. She not only depicts the burden and the anguish but also the hope, the reconciliation, and the healing process. The reader observes Keri regaining control and perspective as she steps toward acceptance and toward restoring health to oneself and one's family. Campbell argues:

> We need to give up the closet regarding mental illness. There is help available, but only if folks admit they need it. In the novel, Keri and Trina both realize that there are no quick fixes for Trina's bipolar disorder, but that if it is managed, she can have a full life. It's critical that people with mental illness obtain a correct diagnosis. Proper medication can manage many symptoms.[55]

*72 Hour Hold* articulates the personal and emotional journey, the shortcomings and issues within the health care system and law enforcement, and the shame, stigma, and denial of African American parents coping with adult children who have mental illness.

In conjunction with the efforts of NULA, Campbell's last novel exemplifies the value of narrative writing and creative production as an activist tool. *72 Hour Hold* travels across distance and expands the local efforts of NULA, thus strengthening the national reach of NAMI. Her literary contribution to this activist work parallels the connection between participation in the Black Action Society during her college years and the rich sociopolitical commentary rendered in *Your Blues Ain't Like Mine*. In all instances she demonstrates a commitment to the greater good of society by working for institutional change, shared healing, and personal transformation. Campbell emerges as a figure who is at once gifted, charismatic, effective, and strategic. Her profound use of enslavement as a metaphor for mental illness drives home her significance as a leading writer of the contemporary period. In the final novel before her death, Campbell clearly lays to rest any question of her literary value. With her precise sociopolitical discourse ensconced in excellent narrative fiction, Bebe Moore Campbell compels and inspires popular audiences and simultaneously has firmly established herself within the American literary canon.

# Epilogue

*The idea is to write it so that people hear it and it slides through the brain and goes straight to the heart.*
—Maya Angelou

In this volume I have endeavored to create an intellectual biography by interpolating two examples of Bebe Moore Campbell's activism and two respective literary works that demonstrate her commitment to sociopolitical change and commentary. The implications of Campbell's literary, activist, and personal legacies are plentiful, especially when her activism with the University of Pittsburgh's Black Action Society (BAS) is juxtaposed with the subsequent release of her first novel, *Your Blues Ain't Like Mine* (1992). Campbell's intentionality is further evidenced by the continuity of her activist work for mental health awareness and advocacy and her final novel, *72 Hour Hold* (2005). Campbell's literary and lived activism moves through a process of frame theory in which she bridges—or effectively introduces a cause, issue, or concern; amplifies—or draws people to become invested or get involved; extends—or broadens the focus to include other related causes; and finally transforms—or changes their viewpoint by introducing and getting people to consider a distinctly different position or set of ideas that advance a social cause. This movement through the framing process is a function of her unique style of bridge leadership that proves effective in her lifelong work toward sociopolitical change.

Not long after the 2005 release of *72 Hour Hold*, Campbell and her loved ones would face devastating news. In February 2006 Campbell was diagnosed with terminal brain cancer with little hope for recovery. By the end of that year, Campbell succumbed to the cancer and died on November 26, 2006. Her premature departure, at the age of fifty-six, leaves us to imagine the future directions her life, work, and career might have taken. *72 Hour Hold* would turn out to be her last novel project, but she would complete two more children's books in addition to *Sometimes My Mommy Gets Angry* (2003). Her husband, Ellis Gordon, notes that she'd begun a sixth novel while she was ailing.[1] He shared that Campbell desired to continue her work with the cause of mental health awareness but also wanted to venture into new directions, including teaching at the university level. She was an active community member, so it would have been easy for her to identify and take on other areas and issues that needed attention and advocacy.

While she was still able to travel, she attended a few speaking engagements and special events to support her alma mater, the University of Pittsburgh. During this time, she was awarded an honorary doctorate to add to her role as an alumni trustee of the university. As the cancer advanced, she spent most of her time resting at home and savoring time with her granddaughter and loved ones. In September 2006 friends and family gathered once more to celebrate life with Bebe, honoring her love of music and dancing with a special luncheon, Bebe's Noon Time Jam.[2] Guests traveled to Los Angeles to visit with Campbell once more following her abrupt diagnosis. Her last nine months must have surely been a most difficult time for the writer, her family, and her friends. Amid the pain of physical illness she remained true to form and found purpose within the somber circumstances of her neurological condition. Campbell made a charge to her friends to collaborate on an essay collection about living and loving someone with cancer. Yet as she convalesced, Campbell remained consistent with the spirited and joy-filled way that she lived her life.

During her final days, Campbell and her daughter, Maia, remained estranged; her daughter struggled with mania, addiction, and living on the street. In November 2012, at age thirty-six, Maia shared her story and agreed to intervention coaching with Iyanla Vanzant on the television show *Fix My Life*.[3] In this heart-wrenching episode, Maia is living in a residential treatment facility and comes to terms with the difficulty she has experienced living with bipolar disorder. She details her feelings of shame, the hardship of living on the streets, and her struggles with sex, drugs, and addictions that complicated her experience with mental illness. She also talks about difficulties and feelings of pressure in her relationship with her mother. Vanzant, who also knew her mother, challenges her to take responsibility and confront her demons in order to start the healing process and find a greater sense of agency. Maia admitted to wanting her mother's attention and approval—wanting to be just like her. She expressed feeling like Campbell put her work first, and Vanzant helps Maia process her love-hate feelings and her loneliness and desperation within the family.

Midway through the episode Maia moves toward forgiveness in a conversation with a life-size photograph of herself and then one of Bebe Moore Campbell. Vanzant then brings Maia's daughter, stepfather, and other family members on the show for processing and healing work. The episode ends with Maia beginning to take ownership for substance abuse problems and proactive care of her mental health and well-being. She talked through "not feeling good enough" and disappointing her parents and her daughter. Since the show aired, she moved from the facility to independent living and spends more time with her daughter. Maia Campbell has shared her story in public speaking engagements and uses social media as a platform for reconnecting with her fan base and exploring new acting projects. The show represented a positive turn in Maia's public life and marked the end of negative coverage and videos of her shoplifting, experiencing manic rants, sex tapes, and other difficult moments when she was unmedicated and living on the streets. While Bebe Moore Campbell did not live to see this transformation, it is uncanny that her daughter moved through surrender, acceptance, healing, and forgiveness, which the writer theorized and depicted in her novels.

As we have learned, Campbell attended the University of Pittsburgh during a very crucial moment in history. Within the BAS, she functioned in several capacities as the students organized and protested for an increase in the number of black students and faculty on campus, a black studies program, a library collection, and more diverse courses. As a young woman, she tutored incoming students, wrote for campus publications, strategized BAS actions within the Political Action Committee, and organized black female students in the BAS affiliate group Black Women for Black Men (BWFBM). Although she did not emerge as a prominent leader or spokesperson, a closer look at the politics of gender-integrated social movements of the 1960s clarifies that formal leadership positions were primarily the domain of men. Nonetheless, Campbell and other young women emerged as leaders in less obvious ways, which were in fact crucial to group success. Her peers remember her as confident, intelligent, and charismatic. These personal traits, along with her inclination toward teaching and writing, advanced organizational goals despite any remnants of the gendered hierarchies articulated within black nationalism. As an informal "bridge" leader, Campbell used multiple vehicles to support change at the grassroots level of the BAS. The cultural pride and the politicization that mark this period in African American history would remain with Campbell throughout her life. In an act of frame shifting, Campbell's first novel, *Your Blues Ain't Like Mine*, would engage readers in the history of the American South and the impact and violence of lynching, but also explore themes of gender, racism, forgiveness, and healing. By revisiting the topics of race, violence, history, and culture, Campbell engages in frame bridging and frame amplification, introducing her readership to some of the sociopolitical ideas that were important and consistent with her involvement in the BAS. However, she also performs frame extension and frame transformation by shifting the medium from organizational activism to literature. She also adds new themes such as forgiveness and healing, compassionate portrayals of white characters, and black women's narratives. These foci are not associated with the black nationalist sentiment of her organizing years with the BAS. The novel *Your Blues Ain't Like Mine* would bridge new themes and new audiences that extended the racial discourse and political ideas of her college years, thus reflecting her growth and maturation.

In her mid-forties and well into a successful writing career, Campbell became involved in another social movement that was, in many ways, distinct from her involvement in the BAS. Fueled by her personal experience, she joined the efforts to increase mental health awareness and advocate for individuals and families living with mental illness. Campbell was keenly aware of the distinct needs of African Americans and people of color, from the struggle with stigma and shame, to the socioeconomic disparities that impeded quality mental health care and access to resources and support. Working with a small group of women, Campbell's interest in the cause evolved from a mothers' prayer group to training and education with the National Alliance on Mental Illness (NAMI), and eventually the founding of a local affiliate chapter, NAMI Urban Los Angeles (NULA). Campbell committed herself to this cause, becoming a national spokesperson and through NULA provided support groups, workshops, and classes in her local community. Because of her growing success as a novelist, she was able to use her celebrity to garner visibility and resources for the group. She also began to use writing as a tool to advance this cause, beginning with a children's book, then a short play, and eventually her final novel, *72 Hour Hold*. Once again, Campbell effectively amplifies the frame of mental health awareness supporting NULA's efforts with the gripping fictional narrative of *72 Hour Hold*. Thus she is able to effect personal and institutional change as related to this cause. Her local work and national fame make her a formal community bridge leader. Accordingly, the grassroots activist work of NULA supports the local community and reaches broad audiences across great distances.

The following key points contrast Campbell's organizational participation and leadership in the two periods of activism examined in this work. Specific to the BAS:

• The organizational makeup was a gender-integrated African American student group, with a formal hierarchical model of leadership that was predominantly male.
• The group's activism yielded increased black student enrollment on campus, the hiring of black faculty, the African American library collection, and the start of the black studies department. The group also worked to increase the number

of relevant courses, campus events, and activities on black culture, life, and history.
• Campbell's leadership role/style was that of an informal bridge leader with no titled or official position. She provided tutoring and social support, and contributed to strategy and mobilization of the BAS through its Political Action Committee and the subgroup BWFBM.
• Campbell also used her writing and contributed articles for the BAS newspaper; wrote the essay "Black Womanhood Defined" in *Black Students Seize the Power to Define*; and would later build on ideologies from the period in her first novel, *Your Blues Ain't Like Mine*.

Regarding Campbell's work with NULA:

• The family support agency utilized a shared group leadership model and was predominantly female and African American.
• Their goal was to eliminate the stigma of mental illness in communities of color, provide support and resources to underserved communities, and advance policy reform within the mental health care system, court system, and criminal justice system
• In NULA, Campbell was a formal community bridge leader because of her titled position as a founder, treasurer, and support group leader with the local group and a spokesperson touring for the national organization. Additionally, she provided personal support to families and made contributions as a teacher/trainer and fund-raiser.
• Campbell used her writing to extend this work with the novel *72 Hour Hold*, the children's book *Sometimes My Mommy Gets Angry*, and the stage play *Even with the Madness*.

As indicated above, the organizational makeup, leadership structure, and program goals of each activist period vary, but several aspects of Campbell's involvement and activities remain the same. Both organizations have antiracist goals: transforming the intellectual and social experiences of black students at a public university and correcting the stigma and the gaps in mental health awareness and support for people of color. Yet the BAS and NULA differ in other ways. The former functions as a gender-integrated movement with a hierarchical leadership structure and is governed by male officers. The latter group embraces a shared leadership model comprised of families but in effect was predominantly led by women. Campbell's involvement in the BAS often took the form of "autonomous pioneering activities rather than through titled or hierarchical positions."[4] However, within both groups her colleagues remembered her as a swift and excellent thinker who contributed crucial ideas, questions, and strategies to mobilize and forward each organization's goals. In addition to being a very action-oriented person, Campbell used writing as a form of consciousness-raising. From her student writing in the 1960s to her recent published works on mental illness, Campbell has been effective in increasing public interest, drawing in constituents, and amplifying the importance of each cause. With NULA, Campbell also played a key role in fund-raising and increasing the visibility of the group. Social movement theories emphasize the importance of resource mobilization to the success of an organization.[5] Combining her celebrity and her innovation, she was able to enhance NULA's stability as it broadened its operations. Finally, her inclination toward teaching and support manifest both in BAS activities as a tutor and cofounder of BWFBM and with NULA as a workshop and support group facilitator. This avenue is often the site of transformative activism where information is provided and personal experiences and beliefs are examined and challenged.[6] The recurring instances of support, counseling, and learning new information in Campbell's personal and public life suggest a value for self-care and personal growth as a function of institutional change. This position becomes a key feature distinguishing Campbell's activist work and writing.

This work has placed Campbell within the legacy of black women who serve activist causes and led in ways that are typically perceived as ancillary. As Robnett elucidates in her study of black women bridge leaders of the civil rights movement, leaders like Campbell are essential to the success of social movements, organizations, and political causes. Within the BAS and NAMI, Campbell engaged in the groundwork and initial development of the organization. She was recognized as a charismatic personality and was able to utilize a personable one-on-one approach to connect people to each movement. While she was not a formal leader in the earlier group, her value to the BAS was uncontested by male and female colleagues. Later on she was able to experience greater leadership in the nonhierarchical, gender-homogenous structure of NULA. Campbell's leadership and activist style essentially remained the same; however, her impact was broadened by the shift in social context and gender norms from the late 1960s to the late 1990s, the insights drawn from her personal growth and life experiences, her maturation as a professional writer, and a personal investment in establishing a safety net to address the needs of a family member impacted by mental illness.

The two relationships examined in this work provide the opportunity to consider Campbell's activist and accompanying literary work in two distinct periods of her life. The first relationship connects her activist work with the BAS at the University of Pittsburgh (chapter 1) with her literary work and the sociopolitical political commentary of her first novel, *Your Blues Ain't Like Mine* (chapter 3). In the second relationship, Campbell's mental health activism and formation of NULA (chapter 2) is connected to her final novel, *72 Hour Hold* (chapter 4). There are meaningful contrasts, progressions, and continuities from which to glean insight on Campbell's motivations, strategies, and priorities. In both relationships, the signature themes of each novel reflect the sociopolitical realities and experiences of African American people, with a focus on African American women. Also, in both novels and activist periods she meaningfully addresses black-white relationships and creates meaningful white characters with which to explore the tensions, complexities, and alliances across racial lines. A key distinction is that in the first relationship, the interaction between the period of activism and the publication of the novel is sequential rather than concurrent. That is, *Your Blues Ain't Like Mine* was published twenty years after Campbell's graduation from Pitt and involvement with the BAS. Thus it is argued that the novel is informed by and reflects the racial and political consciousness of Campbell's college years, but is not written at the same time. Conversely, *72 Hour Hold* is published deliberately and simultaneous to her work with NULA. Here I examine other similarities and differences.

The relationship between *Your Blues Ain't Like Mine* and the BAS articulates Campbell's general ideas about race and activism, which directly inform her evolving consciousness. In the relationship between *72 Hour Hold* and NULA, the activism precedes the novel as a deliberate extension of the social cause. For Campbell, it is a more conscious act of advocacy and awareness in literary form. Still, in both cases the primary activist work precipitates and informs each literary work. There are also similarities in focus between the two periods. Campbell maintains her interest and investment in race, gender, and African American history and culture. In both instances, she embraces a shared leadership style that emphasizes collective work and community. She is observed as an initiator and motivator, skilled at organizing and gathering people for a meaningful cause. Campbell consistently takes interest in the distinct experiences within each cause while maintaining her commitment and investment in a larger constituency. Thus in the first relationship she is active in the BAS subgroup BWFBM and also writes about black women's gendered experiences in the rural South of the 1950s, 1960s, and 1970s. In the second relationship, she organizes to provide mutual support among a group of women with mentally ill loved ones, and in *72 Hour Hold* she focuses on the specific experience of mothers with mentally ill children. She is able to do this without isolating other identity groups that may find value in her writing and activist work. Also, in both relationships it is obvious that Campbell actively uses writing as a tool of her activism. So although her first novel did not emerge until the 1990s, she actively wrote with sociopolitical themes for newspapers at Pitt and continued after graduation through her career as a freelance journalist. Later in life she offered *72 Hour Hold*, using her craft of writing to innovate and inspire others to consider the cause of mental health awareness.

Expectedly, Campbell's activism with NULA as an experienced adult would differ in some ways from her involvement in the BAS

as a teenager and young adult. While she was active in the founding of each group, Campbell took on a more primary leadership
role with her NAMI cofounders in contrast to the support role she
held in the male-led BAS. As an older woman Campbell possessed
a more precise and exact discourse on black womanhood that
was distinctly antisexist and more mature than the "stand beside
your man" sentiment of her 1960s student essay, "Black Womanhood Defined" in *Black Students Seize the Power to Define* (see
chapter 3). Whereas Campbell's student activism was born out of
the discrimination and disparities faced by black collegians on a
predominantly white campus, her mental health activism reflects
the personal sphere of health, family, and motherhood. Both
efforts held connections with local community and neighborhood
support and extended institutional change. At the University of
Pittsburgh, the BAS effectively negotiated multiple concessions
and improvements for students on campus, and instituted long-
term policies and programs to maintain these changes. Forty
years later the impact can be seen in the diverse student population, the numerous scholarships and avenues of financial support, and the strong coalition of African American alumni who
support the university. Campbell remained involved, sustaining
close ties with the campus and engaging with students, faculty,
administration, and alumni to continue this progress.

Similarly, alongside her colleagues at NULA, Campbell challenged the national organization to increase its outreach to communities of color. She became a national spokesperson for NAMI,
and her writings on mental illness were endorsed as recommended
reading for families. Since then NAMI has had multiple campaigns
that diversify and extend its outreach more broadly. The NULA
team has also taken a central role in lobbying the US Congress for
policy shifts and mental health care reform. They also campaigned
for the inauguration of Bebe Moore Campbell National Minority
Mental Health Month each July. This annual celebration would
help to increase the visibility of this cause. While it might seem
that her impact with NULA is broader and holds greater impact
than with the BAS, her lifelong work extended the impact of her
student years at the University of Pittsburgh, as she became a

distinguished alumna and honorary trustee for her alma mater. Moreover, the collective legacy of the students in the BAS is evident in the diversity and African American progress that the institution now boasts.

Campbell has not been explicitly identified or did not self-identify as a proponent of black feminist thought. Still, there are obvious linkages that reveal Campbell's antisexist strivings across various spheres of her life. She has consistently revealed a "woman-identified" agenda, and interviews with her loved ones confirmed this interest and support of "women's issues."[7] A few participants expressly claimed Campbell as a womanist, to affirm her support of black women and men alike, and to deflect the negative connotations of feminism that prevail in black communities. Nonetheless, by definition, black feminism aligns with Campbell's own strivings to work "alongside and in challenge to black men . . . (but also) in support of black men," not to mention the ideas of standpoint and intersectionality outlined by Collins in the seminal volume *Black Feminist Thought: Knowledge, Consciousness, and the Politics of Empowerment.*[8] This is so much the case that Collins even uses excerpts from Campbell's memoir, *Sweet Summer: Growing Up with and without My Dad*, to elucidate ideas about black women's lived experiences. Campbell's topical focus on motherhood and familial, romantic, and sexual relationships, as well as a wide range of identity politics within her fiction, further evidences her interest in and awareness of the intersections of race, class, and gender. This is critical to establish because Campbell possesses a very pronounced commitment to racial commentary and social criticism and is lauded for the antiracist themes in *Your Blues Ain't Like Mine*. Yet as this antiracist discourse aligns with the black nationalist influences of her college years, the subthemes in her fiction and the examples in her life and activist work clearly evidence a broader range of social and political concerns.

Campbell's diverse political priorities and intellectual concerns are not surprising when placed in context. Bernard Bell offers that the African American novel rests on African oral and literary traditions of the past, and yet is unique for also bringing its own distinctly African American cultural meaning and agenda to a primarily American literary form.[9] Historically, African American literature has done the work of examining the intimacies of black life, history, and culture. African American literature has also been a tool of propaganda for cultivating self-determination, consciousness, and nationalism. Thus African American literature has been a source for ongoing commentary on racism in the United States and the many other social and political conditions experienced by black people. We see this commitment in all of Campbell's writing, particularly in her use of African American historical memory and topics that connect readers to black life and culture.

Likewise, much of Campbell's contemporary writing and activism reflects her coming of age during the 1960s black liberation era and the emergence of the women's liberation movements of the 1970s. The influence of the Black Arts movement and the emergence of black women writers during the late 1960s and early 1970s are both evident in Campbell's writing. One can also see the impact of the black feminist and black liberation movements that predate her writing. She notes Toni Morrison as one of her favorite writers but also was directly influenced by other black writers of the period. While at the University of Pittsburgh, Sonia Sanchez was one of Campbell's professors, and she also enjoyed campus visits from many of the Black Arts movement's leading figures. After college, writing workshops with Toni Cade Bambara and John O. Killens honed her writing and nurtured her confidence at a time when it was difficult for black writers to get published. Thus she can be considered a successor to the legacy of the previous generation of Black Arts movement writers. Along with her Black Arts movement antecedents, black feminist criticism locates Campbell, and black women writers in general, squarely within the African American literary tradition but also gives life to its distinctions. Black feminist criticism considers black women's writing as a narrative rejection of stereotype and a continuation of black folk traditions, and includes themes of spirituality, mother/daughter relationships, and women's relationships with one another.[10] This lens most accurately frames the signature themes in *Your Blues* and *72 Hour Hold* that extend an intersectional antisexist analysis or depart from the concerns of black nationalism. Overall, I would argue that the signature themes I highlight in Campbell's first and final novels are influenced by Campbell's college years situated amid the Black Arts and black nationalist movements, the emergence of black feminist theory, and her early contact with direct study under beacons of the African American literary tradition (Sonia Sanchez, Toni Cade Bambara, John O. Killens).

By exploring Bebe Moore Campbell's narrative through the lens of her intellectual, creative, and activist work, it is clear that sociopolitical contributions are consistent with historical trends in black women's activism. She also adds to this body of work within contemporary black women's activism, particularly the increasing focus on health and wellness activism. Whereas black women's health activism had initially focused on physical issues like breast cancer, HIV/AIDS, sexual health, and heart health, Campbell addresses a major gap with her focus on mental illness. Her activism uses multiple strategies; thus her writing on mental health can be framed within the trend of black women's contemporary media activism, using art and creative work to advance a sociopolitical message. An analysis of primarily female support–based friendship networks and Campbell's commitment to community and family broadens the context of her activism, writing, and life trajectory. A close look at Campbell's life reveals a proclivity for cultivating health and wellness as seen in her insistence on marital counseling, various support groups, spiritual practice, diet, exercise, and rest, an important subtext to Campbell's approach to activism.

Also, Campbell places an emphasis on self-care and healing, which counters an inclination and history of self-sacrifice and neglect on the part of black women and on behalf of their children, their men, and their communities.[11] Campbell's activism is born of personal and communal experiences, drawing from the ordinary or mundane occurrences and issues in her life and around her. Yet her impact is felt on the local and national levels and fosters institutional shifts and policy changes in the United States. Thus her activism is able to affect both the micro and macro levels of change. Campbell offers a model of activism that serves both local and national agendas, prioritizes self-care over self-sacrifice while serving one's community, and utilizes personal gifts and talents to advance a cause. Overall, Campbell's activism has been effective and egoless, with an emphasis on shared leadership structures and mechanisms for personal support. Her example both aligns with the most successful black women activists of the past and serves as a model for continued activism in the contemporary period in the interest of social change. Ultimately, bridge leadership is about building relationships and trust. This inspires people to remain interested and involved in a political issue. Campbell shared this dynamic ability in both her writing and in her personal interaction.

For Bebe Moore Campbell, personal experience and community responsibility merge to create a social concern and political positioning that are followed by actions that challenge social policies and political institutions. Studying the details and motivations of Campbell's work as a black student activist and later as a mental health awareness advocate does more than yield topic data in each of these content areas. Looking at the whys and hows of the causes that she took up can potentially reveal connections, values, trends, and beliefs that extend from her personal beliefs, values, and experiences. There is the opportunity to draw from her example the ways by which our own personal beliefs, values, and experiences can serve as impetus for social action as individuals and our efforts to effect change in our own communities (local, national, or global). The personal and ordinary aspects of social responsibility, and the resulting activism, have the potential to be taken for granted or clouded by seemingly more radical, bolder, and more publicized images of activism. While Campbell utilizes her personal gift of writing as a vehicle for the causes that she values, each of us has the ability to make a personal contribution toward social change. However, one must clearly identify the roles and resources that he or she brings to the table. Campbell was clear about this and about the purpose of her writing.

When asked about her "issue-oriented writing" in *Time* magazine (August 2005), she stated:

> My mother was a social worker, and so I grew up with a lot of social workers for friends. And the era, the backdrop for my life, was the civil-rights movement. So that comes quite naturally to me. To me, there's no point in writing merely to entertain. I have to entertain, because if I don't entertain you, you're not going to continue reading. But if I'm not out to enlighten, or change your mind about something, or change your behavior, then I really don't want to take the journey.[12]

For Campbell, writing was a direct and personal expression of activism and outreach. By her own admission, she seeks not only to entertain her readers but also to transform them.

# Appendix 1

**Interview Participants**

Nancy Carter
Pat Clark
Dr. Jack Daniel
Tony Fountain
Dr. Lynn Goodloe
Ellis Gordon
Francine Outen Greer
Marieta Harper
Barbara Hayden
Luddy Hayden
Dr. Joe McCormick
Karen McKie
Rozalyn McPherson
Doris Moore
Dr. Judi Moore Latta
Ramona Phillips
Sonia Sanchez
Linda Wharton Boyd

# Appendix 2

**Interview Instruments A and B**

*Student Activism at the University of Pittsburgh*

1. What years were you present at the University of Pittsburgh?
2. What was your role at the University? (department, student, faculty, other)
3. What brought you to the University of Pittsburgh?
4. Can you describe the social and political climate in the city of Pittsburgh during 1967–1971?
5. Can you describe the social and political climate on campus during 1967–1971?
6. Can you recall the outcomes or details of student activism or political groups on campus?
7. Did you know (or know of) Bebe Moore while you were at the University of Pittsburgh?

    a. If so, what was your impression of her?

    b. Can you recount any particular memories observing or interacting with her personally (i.e., personal characteristics as a student, classmate, friend)?

    c. Can you recount any particular memories of her service and activism on campus (i.e., activities, programs, leadership strategies and attributes)?

8. Are you familiar with Bebe Moore Campbell's fiction or non-fiction work?
9. Have you read any of them? If so which ones?
10. What is your impression or observation of her written work?
11. Are you familiar with her work with Mental Health advocacy?
12. What is your impression or observation of her advocacy work?
13. What is your overall impression or observation of Bebe Moore Campbell's various works (student activity, writing, mental health advocacy).

*Mental Health Advocacy*

1. Did you know Bebe Moore while she worked with NAMI (National Alliance on Mental Illness)?

    a. If so, in what capacity (co-worker, friend, relative, etc.)

    b. What was your impression of her?

    c. Can you recount any particular memories observing or interacting with her?

    d. When did you meet her (please describe)?

2. Are you familiar with her work with Mental Health advocacy?

3. Can you describe any conversations that you had with her about Mental Health advocacy?

4. Can you recount any Mental Health awareness projects, events, or programs that you observed or participated in with Bebe Moore Campbell?

5. What is your impression or observation of her advocacy work?

6. Are you familiar with Bebe Moore Campbell's fiction or non-fiction work?

7. Have you read any of them? If so which ones?

8. What is your impression or observation of her written work?

9. What is your overall impression or observation of Bebe Moore Campbell's various works (writing, mental health advocacy).

# Notes

## Introduction

1. Book reviews notwithstanding, there are very few scholarly articles that address her literature and even fewer offering any detailed biographical accounts of the author. Campbell's fiction has been included in a few edited volumes on contemporary black fiction, and with entries in reference texts and catalogs of recent black writers. There are also a few theses and dissertations (see theses and dissertations by Amos, Dragoin, Hall, Razza, Soden-Harcum, Tewkesbury, Williams, and Williams-Forson) that include scholarly analysis of her first novel, *Your Blues Ain't Like Mine* (1992), but not as the primary focus. Her memoir, *Sweet Summer: Growing Up with and without My Dad* (1989), details the events of her childhood. This book is the first comprehensive, critical treatment of her life and work in a single work.

2. For example, *Your Blues Ain't Like Mine* is useful in US history classes as it treats the issues of sharecropping, racial violence, and migration. *Singing in the Comeback Choir* is useful in courses on politics and social issues and addresses issues like urban gentrification, at-risk youth, and the elderly.

3. The implication of this statement is that Morrison, one of a handful of black women writers given serious and frequent scholarly consideration by white and black academics alike, has evidenced a canonical validity that Campbell has not. Furthermore the notion that there is room for only one black female literary exemplar is both problematic and hegemonic.

4. Campbell's circle of contemporary black writers included friends and admirers such as esteemed novelists Terry McMillan, E. Lynn Harris, Pearl Cleage, Tina McElroy Ansa, and Patrice Gaines. Her work also received praise from renowned "elders" of the black literary tradition such as Sonia Sanchez, who eulogized Campbell in the public address "The Impact of Bebe Moore Campbell on the African American and American Literary Genre," Legacy Memorial Tribute Dinner, Sheraton Hotel Center City, Philadelphia, April 11, 2008.

5. Patrice Gaines, "A Writer for Our Time: Bebe Moore Campbell, 1950–2006," *Black Issues Book Review* 9 (January/February 2007): 19.

6. David A. Snow, Louis A. Zurcger Jr., and Sheldon Eckland-Olsen, "Frame Alignment Processes, Micromobilization, and Movement Participation," *American Sociological Review* 1, no. 4 (1986): 464–468.

7. Nikol Alexander-Floyd, *Gender, Race, and Nationalism in Contemporary Black Politics* (New York: Palgrave Macmillan, 2007).

8. Paraphrased from Belinda Robnett, *How Long, How Long: African American Women in the Struggle for Civil Rights* (New York: Oxford University Press, 1997), 20.

9. Layli Phillips, *The Womanist Reader: The First Quarter Century of Womanist Thought* (New York: Routledge, 2006).

10. Patricia Hill Collins, *Black Feminist Thought: Knowledge, Consciousness, and the Politics of Empowerment* (New York: Routledge, 1991).

11. Maia Campbell, interview by Iyanla Vanzant on *Fix My Life* (Oprah Winfrey Network), November 17, 2012.

## Chapter One

1. Bebe Moore Campbell, *Sweet Summer: Growing Up with and without My Dad* (New York: G. P. Putnam's Sons, 1989).

2. Ibid., 63.

3. Ibid., 64.

4. Jane Campbell, "An Interview with Bebe Moore Campbell," *Callaloo: A Journal of African-American and African Arts and Letters* 22, no. 4 (Fall 1999): 956.

5. When Campbell was still a baby, Doris and George Moore owned a small restaurant with friends. After a severe accident, he was paralyzed from the waist down and took part-time jobs to support himself and his daughter.

6. Campbell, *Sweet Summer*, 203.

7. Joe McCormick, phone interview by author, November 4, 2009.

8. African American Alumni Council of the Pitt Alumni Association, "Blue, Gold, and Black: The Colors of Celebration, Forty Years of African American Pride, Progress, and Partnership with the University of Pittsburgh," Sankofa Homecoming Weekend 2009 Program Book, October 22–25, 2009.

9. Joy Ann Williamson provides an important case study for documenting 1960s black student activism in *Black Power on Campus: The University of Illinois 1965–1975* (Urbana: University of Illinois Press, 2003). Likewise, Noliwe Rooks provides descriptive detail of black student activism as background and context in *White Money/Black Power: The Surprising History of African American Studies and the Crisis of Race in Higher Education* (Boston: Beacon Press, 2006).

10. Meeting Minutes, June 4, 1968, Black Action Society Archives (UA 55/16/3 A–B), Box 1, Folder 1, Archive Service Center, University of Pittsburgh.

11. Doris Moore, interview by author, Los Angeles, December 11, 2009.

12. See, for example, William L. Van Deburg, *New Day in Babylon: The Black Power Movement and American Culture, 1965–1975* (Chicago: University of Chicago Press, 1992).

13. For a detailed study of SNCC, see Howard Zinn, *SNCC: The New Abolitionists* (Cambridge, Mass.: South End Press, 2002); and Carson Clayborne, *In Struggle: SNCC and the Black Awakening of the 1960s* (Cambridge, Mass.: Harvard University Press, 1995).

14. Van Deburg, *New Day in Babylon*.

15. Ibid.

16. Peniel Joseph, in "Dashikis and Democracy: Black Studies, Student Activism, and the Black Power Movement," *Journal of African American History* 88, no. 2 (2003): 182–203, examines this relationship and recounts a detailed history of the period. In his opening he offers that "contemporary Black Studies programs owe a large, and largely forgotten, debt to radical social movements that resulted in student protest demonstrations across the country." He notes that black radical and nationalist discourse was central to struggles of race, class, and educational and economic opportunity. Joseph traces the black studies movement to an organization called the Afro American Society that began at Merritt Community College. Members formed study groups and think tanks, and continued to organize in the tradition of SNCC and other groups of the period.

17. John Bunzel, "Black Studies at San Francisco State," in *The African American Studies Reader*, ed. Nathaniel Norment Jr., 2nd ed. (Durham, N.C.: Carolina Academic Press, 2007), 255.

18. Rooks, *White Money/Black Power*.

19. The gains at SFSU are notable in part because it was the first successful movement for black studies at a four-year college, but also because Nathan Hare was hired as chair and was active, vocal, and controversial in black higher education at the time. Hare became a formative voice in the structural and theoretical development of the discipline.

20. Rooks, *White Money/Black Power*.

21. Ibid.

22. See also Fabio Rojas, *From Black Power to Black Studies: How a Radical Social Movement Became an Academic Discipline* (Baltimore: Johns Hopkins University Press, 2007).

23. Sonia Sanchez, interview by author, Philadelphia, March 20, 2010.

24. Building on the general accounts of the black studies movement and black student activists, recent scholarship has included critical assessment of this period, its strengths and its failings, and detailed accounts of student

movements on specific campuses. William Exum's *Paradoxes of Protest: Black Student Activism in a White University* (Philadelphia: Temple University Press, 1985) considers the case of University College (a branch of New York University) and investigates the failures and successes of student protest. In *The Black Student Protest Movement at Rutgers* (Newark, N.J.: University of Rutgers Press, 1990), Richard McCormick offers a record of student activism at Rutgers University on its Camden, Newark, and New Brunswick campuses. He confirms the intensified tension on campus following the assassination of Martin Luther King Jr. and the concern of students, both black and white, with antiwar campaigning.

25. Williamson's *Black Power on Campus* is yet another work detailing the black student movement at a particular institution. Framed as a study on the impact of social movements at higher education institutions, Williamson argues for the influences of black student activism on structural change and reform by college administration. She highlights the adoption of Black Power ideology by University of Illinois students to forcefully advance their cause. She includes a list of thirty-five demands made by the Black Student Association on campus, which included concerns for the university's black custodial and service workers, housing discrimination on campus, increased admission, and a black cultural center run by the students. This and other accounts of student struggles on particular campuses provide an intimate look at the nature of black student activism, its ideology, its strivings, and its shortcomings. On each campus there were both commonalities and variations to the black student movement. Collectively, these studies describe and examine the climate of the period, the concerns of young African American college students, and the process of politicization during this period in US history. These studies not only reveal the importance of black student activism but also narrate the similarities and differences of specific campus movements.

26. Linda Wharton Boyd, interview by author, Washington, D.C., March 14, 2009.

27. Demands of the Black Action Society, May 20, 1968, Black Action Society Archives (UA 55/16/3 A–B), Box 1, Folder 1, Archive Service Center, University of Pittsburgh.

28. Black Action Society Meeting Minutes and Program Proposal, June 11, 1968, Black Action Society Archives (UA 55/16/3 A–B), Box 1, Folder 1, Archive Service Center, University of Pittsburgh.

29. *Black Action News* (Student Publication), October 22 and December 1, 1968, Black Action Society Archives (UA 55/16/3 A–B), Box 1, Folder 1, Archive Service Center, University of Pittsburgh. *Black Action News* featured student writing and local and national coverage of police brutality, labor issues, and student activism.

30. Barbara Hayden, interview by author.

31. Wharton Boyd interview.

32. Luddy Hayden, phone interview by author November 10, 2009.

33. Jack Daniel, interview by author, Pittsburgh, October 23, 2009.

34. Paula Giddings, *When and Where I Enter: The Impact of Black Women on Race and Sex in America* (New York: Perennial, 2001), 299–324.

35. Robnett, *How Long, How Long*, 15–20, 190.

36. Ibid., 190.

37. Ibid., 19–20.

38. Tony Fountain, interview by author, October 25, 2009.

39. Robnett, *How Long, How Long*, 15–20, 190.

40. Marita Harper, phone interview by author, November 11, 2009.

41. Ibid.

42. Wharton Boyd interview.

43. Black Action Society, Meeting Minutes for June 4 and June 11, 1968, Black Action Society Archives (UA 55/16/3 A–B), Box 1, Folder 1, Archive Service Center, University of Pittsburgh. Members discussed tutoring programs for new students. Campbell was present at both meetings and was listed as a tutor.

44. Snow, Zurcger, and Eckland-Olsen, "Frame Alignment Processes," 464–468; also cited in Robnett, *How Long, How Long*, 13; and Alexander-Floyd, *Gender, Race, and Nationalism*, 41—43.

45. Wharton Boyd interview.

46. Ibid. See also *Black Action News* (Student Publication), October 15, 1971, Black Action Society Archives (UA 55/16/3 A–B), Box 1, Folder 1, Archive Service Center, University of Pittsburgh.

47. This ideology included an emphasis on nationalism, active political engagement, embracing black cultural identity, independent control of community resources, and a Pan-African connection to black people around the world. The Black Power movement's creative sibling, the Black Arts movement, complements the assertive stance of pro-black articulation, bold critique of systemic injustice, and emphasis on community building. The Black Arts movement, a simultaneous emergence of aesthetic production that rejected Western and mainstream standards of value and beauty in place of a politicized, culturally affirming aesthetic, harvested an abundance of literature, visual art, music, theater, and dance during the period.

48. The program was named for American civil rights leader Martin Luther King Jr., black nationalist leader Malcolm X, and Jamaican cultural nationalist leader Marcus Garvey.

49. Meeting Minutes, June 4 and June 11, 1968, Black Action Society Archives (UA 55/16/3 A–B), Box 1, Folder 1, Archive Service Center, University of Pittsburgh.

50. Demands of the Black Action Society, May 20, 1968, Black Action Society Archives (UA 55/16/3 A–B), Box 1, Folder 1, Archive Service Center, University of Pittsburgh.

51. Kenneth Schuler to Black Action Society, June 21, 1968, Student Activities (UA 55/7/1), Box 6, Folder 62, Archive Service Center, University of Pittsburgh; *Pitt News*, June 28, 1968, Black Action Society Archives (UA 55/16/3 A–B), Box 1, Folder 1, Archive Service Center, University of Pittsburgh. Students were given temporary status as a student organization, campus publications espoused support of the group, and the university hired a new black faculty member to lead the University Community Education Program (UCEP).

52. Hayden interview.

53. African American Alumni Council of the Pitt Alumni Association, "Blue, Gold, and Black."

54. Black Action Society, Meeting Minutes for June 4, 1968, Black Action Society Archives (UA 55/16/3, A–B), Box 1, Folder 1, Archive Service Center, University of Pittsburgh; *Pitt News*, June 28, 1968, Black Action Society Archives (UA 55/7/1), Box 6, Folder 62, Archive Service Center, University of Pittsburgh.

55. Steven Davis, "Black Students and Graduate Study at the University of Pittsburgh," n.d., Black Action Society Archives (UA 55/16/3 A–B), Box 1, Folder 1, Archive Service Center, University of Pittsburgh.

56. Lloyd Bell to Bernard Kobosky, Memorandum, January 9, 1970, Associate Dean, Office Files, Division of Natural Sciences (UA 90/4/2/1), Box 6, Folder 62, Archive Service Center, University of Pittsburgh.

57. *Pitt News*, January 16, 1969, Black Action Society Archives (UA 55/7/1), Box 6, Folder 62, Archive Service Center, University of Pittsburgh.

58. William Markus and John Vrana to Jack Critchfied and Dean Ronald Pease, Memorandum, June 26, 1968, Associate Dean, Office Files, Division of Natural Sciences (UA 90/4/2/1), Box 6, Folder 62, Archive Service Center, University of Pittsburgh.

59. David Halliday to Dean Richard McCoy, November 23, 1968, Associate Dean, Office Files, Division of Natural Sciences (UA 90/4/2/1), Box 6, Folder 62, Archive Service Center, University of Pittsburgh.

60. Meeting Minutes, Study Group for University Program for Culturally Deprived Students, January 30, 1968, Associate Dean, Office Files, Division of Natural Sciences (UA 90/4/2/1), Box 6, Folder 62, Archive Service Center, University of Pittsburgh.

61. Black Action Society to Chancellor Wesley Posvar, November 29, 1968, Black Action Society Archives (UA 55/16/3), Box 1, Folder 1, Archive Service Center, University of Pittsburgh.

62. Wharton Boyd interview.

63. *Black Action News*, December 1, 1968, Black Action Society Archives (UA 55/7/1), Box 6, Folder 62, Archive Service Center, University of Pittsburgh; Campbell pens the headline story about labor issues in California, "BAS Supports Grape Boycott," *Black Action News*, March 23, 1970, Black Action Society Archives (UA 55/7/1), Box 6, Folder 62, Archive Service Center, University of Pittsburgh; Campbell is listed as staff writer and pens article on the Black Church, Black Action Society Archives (UA 55/7/1), Box 6, Folder 62, Archive Service Center, University of Pittsburgh; *Pitt News*, June 28, 1968, Black Action Society Archives (UA 55/7/1), Box 6, Folder 62, Archive Service Center, University of Pittsburgh.

64. Daniel interview.

65. The other essay in the publication, by Martha Carson, is titled "Black Manhood Defined." Risking criticism for attempting to "define" black manhood, Carson presses forward, and she too supplants a concealed imperative for men, while on the surface maintaining the black nationalist patriarchy. For Carson, black manhood is about fatherhood, leadership, and community responsibility. However, she also challenges black men on issues of parenthood, sexual indiscretion, and aspiring to white patriarchal models of material success.

66. Elizabeth Moore and Martha Carson, *Black Students Seize the Power to Define*, undated student publication, Black Action Society Archives (UA 55/16/3 A-B), Box 1, Folder 1, Archive Service Center, University of Pittsburgh. The second essay in the document, written by Martha Carson, explores redefining black manhood.

67. Ibid.

68. Stefan Bradley's "'Gym Crow Must Go!' Black Student Activism at Columbia University, 1967–1968," *Journal of African American History* 88, no. 2 (2003): 163–181, provides an in-depth narrative of the black students' protest against the university's erecting a new gymnasium between the campus and the local Harlem community in April 1969. He highlights student protest activity, the influence of Black Power ideology, and the interactions and tensions between white and black student activists on campus. In addition to political demonstrations such as sit-ins, strikes, and protests, campus activists added to their strategies the barricading and occupying of buildings, and holding administrators and faculty captive. At Columbia, the proposal of the new gym represented encroachment into the local black and Puerto Rican communities, who were virtually denied access to the new campus facility in their neighborhood. The students took over Hamilton Hall, a classroom and administrative building, and eventually forced the white student activists to exit the building due to differences in strategy. Over several days various black and white student groups protested and demonstrated across campus. The black

students' protest was swelled in number with the support of local activists, community members, white student groups, and some faculty groups. The Columbia protest ended in a police standoff; however, the university conceded and ceased plans to build a gym over Harlem Heights's Morningside Park.

69. Hayden interview.

70. *Pitt News*, January 16, 1969, Black Action Society Archives (UA 55/7/1), Box 6, Folder 62, Archive Service Center, University of Pittsburgh; *Pitt News*, June 28, 1968, Black Action Society Archives (UA 55/7/1), Box 6, Folder 60.

71. *Pitt News*, January 16, 1969, Black Action Society Archives (UA 55/7/1), Box 6, Folder 62, Archive Service Center, University of Pittsburgh.

72. Francine Outen Greer, interview by author, Atlanta, May 8, 2009.

73. The students negotiated the following demands: the assurance that no punitive action would be taken against the students; the appointment of a black recruitment officer; recruitment of additional black faculty, administrators, and personnel; the opening of an African American collection at Hilman Library; the institution of and funding for a black studies program with directors appointed by June 1969; and the acknowledgment of Martin Luther King Jr.'s birthday as a university holiday, and February 21, Malcolm X's birthday, as an excused day for the black students, faculty, administrators, and staff.

74. Demands of the Black Action Society, May 20, 1968, Black Action Society Archives (UA 55/16/3 A–B), Box 1, Folder 1, Archive Service Center, University of Pittsburgh.

75. Pat Clark, interview by author, Atlanta, May 8, 2009.

76. Common strategies for student activists of the period included staging protests, barricading and occupying buildings on campus, embracing Black Power ideology and rhetoric, and a direct response to racial tensions on campus. See Bradley, 'Gym Crow Must Go!'" See also Williamson, *Black Power on Campus*.

77. Pat Clark, interview by author, May 8, 2009.

78. Greer interview.

79. Ibid.

80. Ibid.

81. Wharton Boyd interview.

82. Ibid.

83. Sanchez interview.

84. McCormick interview.

85. Ibid.

86. Although these students demonstrated an antisexist consciousness reflecting black feminist thought and third wave feminism, some study participants sought to emphasize that Campbell and the work of BWFBM should be labeled womanist, not feminist. Nikol Alexander-Floyd and Evelyn Simien,

in "What's in a Name?: Exploring the Contours of Africana Womanist Thought," *Frontiers: A Journal of Women Studies* 27, no. 1 (2006): 67–89, offer a thorough analysis of this tension around naming and the importance of clarifying antisexist theory and discourse rather than being preoccupied with labels.

87. Daniel interview

88. Campbell, *Sweet Summer*, 213, 239. Campbell tells about advice when a high school boyfriend is pressuring her to have sex before she is ready. Later, a father figure gives her "the talk" and advises her to be safe and make sure that she is feeling good about intercourse despite any "sweet talk" college guys may offer.

89. Toni Cade's anthology *The Black Woman* (New York: Signet 1970) gathers the perspectives of black women thinkers during the 1960s and 1970s. See also Mahdu Dubey, *Black Women Novelists and the Nationalist Aesthetic* (Bloomington: Indiana University Press, 1994).

90. The first female president, Ramona Riscoe, was elected in 1979, and there have been several women elected since then. This is important given the active participation and leadership of black female students in the Black Action Society, particularly because of the gendered trends of black male spokespersons and elected leaders in student organizations and activist groups of the 1960s.

91. Although refusing to take credit, Daniel is certainly one of those "community anchors" who has been central to the development of special scholarships. He has submitted studies on African American student needs and programs on campus to the university chancellor, and garners a diverse hiring record across race and gender. He has functioned in multiple administrative positions spanning over four decades in service to the university. Accordingly, for his contributions to the strong legacy of African Americans at Pitt, the Jack L. Daniel Endowed Book Fund was announced during the Sankofa Homecoming Celebration as a part of a new $3 million campaign, which includes the African American Alumni Council Endowed Fund for financial support to underrepresented students.

92. Robnett, *How Long, How Long*, 13.

93. Dubey, *Black Women Novelists*. Dubey details the nature of black women's rejection and acceptance of various components of black nationalist discourse during the 1960 and 1970s.

94. A version of Sanchez's "The Black Woman" syllabus from the 1970s is published in Gloria T. Hull, Patricia B. Scott, and Barbara Smith's seminal work, *All the Women Are White, All the Blacks Are Men, But Some of Us Are Brave* (New York: Feminist Press, 1982), 349.

95. Kimberly Springer, in *Still Lifting Still Climbing* (New York: NYU Press, 1999), addresses the spectrum of black women's self-identification with or distance from the label of feminist but effectively gathers and organizes

accounts of struggle and activism endeavored by black women across the perspective of class, ideology, and political affiliation.

96. Campbell, *Sweet Summer*, 244.

97. Ibid.

98. Ibid., 245.

99. Ellis Gordon, interview by author, Los Angeles, December 10, 2009; Moore interview.

## Chapter Two

1. Bebe Moore Campbell, interview by Ashok Gangadean (*Global Lens*), February, 5, 2006, http://www.consciousnessprecedesmind.org/global-lens-channel/bebe-moore-campbell.html.

2. *Your Blues Ain't Like Mine* received the New York Times Notable Book of the Year and the NAACP Image Award for Literature.

3. Gordon interview.

4. Ibid.

5. Ibid.

6. http://www1.essence.com/news_entertainment/news/articles/maia_campbell_father_and_grandmother_speak_out.

7. Gordon interview.

8. Campbell, interview by Gangadean.

9. McCormick interview.

10. Wharton Boyd interview.

11. Ibid.

12. Nancy Carter, interview by author, Los Angeles, December 11, 2009; Lynn Goodloe, interview by author, Los Angeles, December 13, 2009; Gordon interview; "About NAMI Urban LA," National Alliance on Mental Illness, Urban Los Angeles affiliate, http://www.namiurbanla.org/content/view/13/29/.

13. Campbell was a regular guest on the *Tom Joyner Morning Show* and also held a regular spot on National Public Radio's *Morning Edition*.

14. Carter interview.

15. Kenneth Meeks, "With Bebe Moore Campbell," *Black Enterprise*, April 2006, http://www.blackenterprise.com/2006/04/01/with-bebe-moore-campbell/.

16. Carter interview.

17. Ibid.

18. Ibid.

19. Ibid.

20. Robnett, *How Long, How Long*, 22.

21. Goodloe interview.

22. Ibid.

23. Ibid.

24. Ibid.

25. Ibid.

26. Carter interview; Goodloe interview; Gordon interview.

27. Gordon interview.

28. Robnett, *How Long, How Long*, 22.

29. Goodloe interview.

30. "About NAMI Urban—LA," National Alliance on Mental Illness, Urban Los Angeles affiliate.

31. Ibid.

32. Gordon interview.

33. See Surgeon General's report, http://www.surgeongeneral.gov/library/mentalhealth/cre/.

34. Ibid.

35. Deborah J. Garretson, "Psychological Misdiagnosis of African Americans," *Journal of Multicultural Counseling & Development* 21, no. 2 (1993): 122.

36. F. M. Baker, "Diagnosing Depression in African Americans," *Community Mental Health Journal* 37, no. 1 (2001): 31; Diane R. Brown and Feroz Ahmed, "Major Depression in a Community Sample of African Americans," *American Journal of Psychiatry* 152, no. 3 (1995): 373.

37. Carter interview.

38. Ibid.

39. The formal term for a person with mental illness, as in "a consumer of mental health services and support."

40. Robnett, *How Long, How Long*, 22.

41. "Programs and Groups," National Alliance on Mental Illness, Urban Los Angeles affiliate, http://www.namiurbanla.org/content/view/13/29/.

42. Goodloe interview.

43. Ibid.

44. "Resources," National Alliance on Mental Illness, Urban Los Angeles affiliate, http://www.namiurbanla.org/content/view/13/29/.

45. Carter interview.

46. Goodloe interview.

47. Ibid.

48. Ibid.

49. "Mental Health Advocacy Group Critical of Lack of NIMH Research," *Brown University Psychopharmacology Update* 11, no. 2 (2000): 2.

50. Ibid.

51. Ibid.

52. "Statement of Nancy Carter on Behalf of National Alliance on Mental Illness," National Alliance on Mental Illness, http://www.nami.org/Content/ContentGroups/Policy/Issues_Spotlights/Housing4/Nancy_Carter_Test_Homelessness_10.16.07.pdf.

53. Friends and supporters lobbied local, state, and federal politicians to acknowledge July as an annual marker for promoting mental health awareness in communities of color, eventually leading to the inauguration of Bebe Moore Campbell National Minority Mental Health Month in 2007.

54. Goodloe interview.

55. Carla Adkinson-Bradley et al., "Forging a Collaborative Relationship Between the Black Church and the Counseling Profession," *Counseling & Values* 49, no. 2 (2005): 148–149.

56. Ibid.

57. Carter interview.

58. "Thank You, Bebe Moore Campbell," Statement of Michael Fitzpatrick, NAMI Executive Director, November 28, 2006, http://www.nami.org/Content/ContentGroups/Press_Room1/2006/Press_November_2006/Thank_You,_Bebe_Moore_Campbell.htm.

59. "Multicultural Action Network," National Alliance on Mental Illness, http://www.nami.org/Content/ContentGroups/Multicultural_Support1/About_the_NAMI_Multicultural_Action_Center.htm.

60. Carter interview.

61. Gary Lee, "Los Angeles' Black Pride: Taking in the Retro Vibe of Leimert Park," *Washington Post*, March 19, 2006.

62. Carter interview.

63. Ibid.

64. Robnett, *How Long, How Long*, 21.

65. Ibid., 34

**Chapter Three**

1. In addition to being an active alumna, Campbell served as a keynote speaker on multiple occasions, received an honorary doctorate, and served as a trustee of the University of Pittsburgh. At the Sankofa Homecoming Celebration, the African American Alumni Council launched a $3 million fund-raising campaign to support diversity on campus. The Bebe Moore Campbell Endowed Memorial Scholarship Fund was inaugurated as a part of this

initiative. African American Alumni Council of the Pitt Alumni Association, "Blue, Gold, and Black."

2. Campbell began her writing career contributing articles to *Essence, Black Enterprise*, the *Washington Post*, and other notable publications. She was also a member of the National Association of Black Journalists.

3. As discussed in chapter 2, Campbell wrote for the *Black Action News* and expressed an early interest and inclination for writing during her college years.

4. Campbell always held a strong desire to write fiction, but was contracted to publish two nonfiction works first. Gordon interview; Moore interview.

5. Snow, Zurcger, and Eckland-Olsen, "Frame Alignment Processes," 464–468.

6. Ibid.; also cited in Robnett, *How Long, How Long*, 13; and Alexander-Floyd, *Gender, Race, and Nationalism*, 41—43.

7. Campbell, "Interview with Bebe Moore Campbell," 956.

8. Black youth were often the symbols of and participants in civil rights protest. The murder of Emmett Till in 1955 created an uproar across the United States and abroad when *JET* magazine (September 15, 1955) published a photograph of the boy's mutilated body. The coverage of Till's death and the murder trial became a catalyst for increased campaigns for civil rights and equality. In 1963 the bombing of the Sixteenth Street Birmingham Church left four young girls dead in Birmingham, Alabama, and reenergized the struggle against racism and violence in the American South. These bombings were an attempt to discourage local youth and schoolchildren from organizing and protesting segregation in Birmingham.

9. The US sharecropping system was an exploitative practice in which poor African Americans in the South worked the land of former plantation owners and were allowed to keep a portion of the proceeds. Most often black families were cheated and overcharged for rent, supplies, and crop losses, thus remaining in the cycle of poverty. For a detailed discussion, see Elizabeth Nan Woodruff, *American Congo: The African American Freedom Struggle in the Delta* (Cambridge, Mass.: Harvard University Press, 2003); and R. Douglas Hurt, *African American Life in the Rural South, 1900–1950* (Columbia: University of Missouri Press, 2003).

10. See note 9.

11. See note 9.

12. Bebe Moore Campbell, *Your Blues Ain't Like Mine* (New York: G. P. Putnam's Sons, 1992), 308.

13. Ibid.

14. Ibid., 318.

15. Ibid.

16. See Ronald W. Walters, *White Nationalism/Black Interests: Conservative Public Policy and the Black Community*, (Detroit: Wayne State University Press, 2003).

17. The social phenomenon and history of criminalization of African Americans in the urban North is examined in Khalil Gibran Muhammed, *The Condemnation of Blackness: Race, Crime and the Making of Modern Urban America* (Cambridge, Mass.: Harvard University Press, 2003).

18. Campbell, *Your Blues Ain't Like Mine*, 81–82.

19. Ibid., 150.

20. Bebe Moore Campbell, interview by Yvette Gardner, "A Conversation with Bebe Moore Campbell," prologue of *Your Blues Ain't Like Mine*.

21. Campbell, *Your Blues Ain't Like Mine*, 180.

22. Ibid., 203–204.

23. See Angela Johnson-Fisher, *Afristocracy: Free Women of Color and the Politics of Race, Class, and Culture* (VDM Verlag, 2008).

24. Moore and Carson, *Black Students Seize the Power to Define*.

25. Campbell, *Your Blues Ain't Like Mine*, 88.

26. Ibid., 25.

27. Ibid., 78.

28. Ibid.

29. Ibid.

30. Ibid., 12–13.

31. Ibid., 40.

32. Ibid., 13.

33. Ibid.

34. Ibid., 34.

35. Ibid., 30.

36. Giddings, *When and Where I Enter*, 54.

37. Campbell, interview by Gardner.

38. For discussions of the lynching of black men for the alleged rape of white women, see Giddings, *When and Where I Enter*, 26–31; Alfreda M. Duster and Ida B. Wells, *Crusade for Justice: The Autobiography of Ida B. Wells* (Chicago: University of Chicago Press, 1970); and the chapter "The Myth of the Black Rapist" in Angela Davis, *Race, Women, and Class* (New York: Random House, 1981).

39. Moore and Carson, *Black Students Seize the Power to Define*.

40. W. E. B. Du Bois, in the 1935 publication *Black Reconstruction*, offers a Marxist critique of US enslavement and Reconstruction, including an examination of the violent sexual oppression of black women as producers of slave labor. Campbell's treatment of black women's racialized gender position reflects this intersectional analysis and that of black feminist scholars as well.

41. Campbell, interview by Gardner.

42. Snow, Zurcger, and Eckland-Olsen, "Frame Alignment Processes," 464–468; also cited in Robnett, *How Long, How Long*, 13; and Alexander-Floyd, *Gender, Race, and Nationalism*, 41—43.

43. Campbell, *Your Blues Ain't Like Mine*, 285–286.

44. Ibid., 325–326.

45. Ibid., 312.

46. Campbell, interview by Gardner.

47. Ibid.

## Chapter Four

1. Ellis and Bebe have two granddaughters, each of them born to their son and daughter and their respective spouses.

2. Campbell states in various interviews that the book is not about her own life.

3. Campbell, interview by Gangadean.

4. Margo V. Perkins, *Autobiography as Activism: Three Black Women of the Sixties* (Jackson: University Press of Mississippi, 2000), 10, 30.

5. Bipolar disorder (also known as manic depression) is a brain disease that manifests in extreme shifts in moods, energy, and functioning. It is chronic and lifelong and requires treatment to manage cycles of mania and depression. www.nami.org.

6. That is, *The Soloist*, a 2009 film starring Jamie Foxx, depicts the real-life story of a homeless man, Nathaniel Ayers, living with mental illness who is also a skilled violinist.

7. Bebe Moore Campbell, *72 Hour Hold* (New York: Anchor Books, 2006), 133.

8. Ibid., 8.

9. Ibid., 137.

10. Ibid.

11. Ibid., 31.

12. Ibid., 49.

13. Alexander-Floyd, *Gender, Race, and Nationalism*, 41–43.

14. In psychology, the concept of racial memory is associated with Carl Jung and describes feelings and ideas inherited from our ancestors as a part of a "collective unconscious." It extends from the concept of genetic memory, which is memory absent of a sensory experience, encoded in genomes over a long period of time. A. S. Reber and E. Reber, *Penguin Journal of Psychology*, 3rd ed. (New York: Penguin, 2002). In African American culture, this can be associated with historical moments like the Middle Passage and enslavement.

15. Tubman is best known for her escape and her heroic efforts to free hundreds of enslaved African Americans on a series of strategic trips known as the Underground Railroad.

16. Tatiana Morales, "Being on '72 Hour Hold': Bebe Moore Campbell's Novel About Mental Illness," CBS news (online), August 1, 2005, http://www.cbsnews .com/stories/2005/08/01/earlyshow/leisure/books/main713145.shtml?tag=curre ntVideoInfo;videoMetaInfo.

17. The Middle Passage reference denotes the harsh and devastating forced migration of the transatlantic slave trade that followed the capture of indigenous Africans and preceded the sale of captives into chattel slavery. The Middle Passage describes travel by sea for months at a time, primarily in shackles amid severe illness, high death rates, and the regular occurrence of physical, psychological, and sexual violence.

18. Campbell, *72 Hour Hold*, 28.

19. Ibid., 32.

20. Giddings, *When and Where I Enter*, 33–46.

21. Campbell, *72 Hour Hold*, 26.

22. Ibid., 29.

23. Ibid., 33.

24. Ibid., 119.

25. Ibid., 165.

26. Collins examines such themes and complexities in *Black Feminist Thought*. Coincidentally, she makes multiple references to Campbell's autobiography, *Sweet Summer*, to explore some of these themes.

27. Giddings, *When and Where I Enter*, 325–336.

28. Collins, *Black Feminist Thought*, 76.

29. Ibid.

30. Campbell, *72 Hour Hold*, 30.

31. Ibid., 132.

32. Ibid., 30.

33. Ibid., 40.

34. Ibid., 28–29.

35. Ibid.

36. Ibid., 92–93.

37. Collins, *Black Feminist Thought*, 119.

38. Campbell, *72 Hour Hold*, 172.

39. Ibid., 183.

40. Ibid., 217.

41. Ibid., 107.

42. Ibid., 33.

43. Ibid., 242–243.

44. Ibid.

45. Ibid.

46. Ibid.

47. Ibid., 225.

48. Ibid.

49. Ibid., 226.

50. Ibid., 301.

51. Ibid., 314.

52. Ibid., 318.

53. Ibid., 319.

54. Campbell, interview by Gangadean.

55. Quoted in "Thank You, Bebe Moore Campbell," Statement of Michael Fitzpatrick, NAMI Executive Director, November 28, 2006, http://www.nami .org/Content/ContentGroups/Press_Room1/2006/Press_November_2006/ Thank_You,_Bebe_Moore_Campbell.htm.

## Epilogue

1. Gordon interview.

2. Bebe's Noontime Jam: An Exclusive Afternoon of Fun, Friendship and Love with Bebe Moore Campbell, Program Book, Los Angeles, September 23, 2006.

3. *Fix My Life*, Season 1, Episode 12, "Fix My Celebrity Life," aired on November 13, 2012.

4. Robnett, *How Long, How Long*, 21.

5. Ibid., 12.

6. Ibid., 29, 198.

7. Wharton Boyd interview.

8. Collins, *Black Feminist Thought*, 21–22.

9. Bernard Bell, *The Afro American Novel and Its Tradition* (Amherst: University of Massachusetts Press, 1987).

10. See works by Barbara Christian, *African American Women Novelists* (Westport, Conn.: Greenwood Press, 1980), and *Black Feminist Criticism: Perspectives on Women Writers* (New York: Pergamon Press, 1985). See also Dubey, *Black Women Novelists*.

11. Kimberly Springer, *Living for the Revolution, Black Feminist Organizations, 1968–1980* (Durham, N.C.: Duke University Press, 2006), 148. Springer discusses activist burnout as a factor in the decline of black feminist organizations, noting

the "high social costs of activism" and that intense political work was difficult to sustain over long periods of time.

12. Andrea Sachs, "Between the Lines with Bebe Moore Campbell," *Time* (online), August 6, 2005.

# Bibliography

Adksion-Bradley, Carla, et al. "Forging a Collaborative Relationship Between the Black Church and the Counseling Profession." *Counseling & Values* 49, no. 2 (2005): 147–154.

Alexander-Floyd, Nikol. *Gender, Race, and Nationalism in Contemporary Black Politics.* New York: Palgrave Macmillan, 2007.

Alexander-Floyd, Nikol, and Evelyn Simien. "What's in a Name?: Exploring the Contours of Africana Womanist Thought." *Frontiers: A Journal of Women Studies* 27, no. 1 (2006): 67–89.

Amos, Sharon L. Richardson. "Whose Dust Is Rising? Historical and Literary Narratives of the Northern Migration of African American Women." PhD diss., State University of New York at Buffalo, 2005.

Anderson, Keisha-Gaye. "Not Just Singing the Blues." *Black Enterprise* 35, no. 1 (2004): 102–108.

Ani, Marimba. *Yurugu: An African-Centered Critique of European Cultural Thought and Behavior.* Trenton, N.J.: Africa World Press, 1994.

Ayalon, Liat, and Jennifer Alvidrez. "The Experience of Black Consumers in the Mental Health System—Identifying Barriers to and Facilitators of Mental Health Treatment Using the Consumers' Perspective." *Issues in Mental Health Nursing* 28, no. 12 (2007): 1323–1340.

Azibo, Daudi A. "Articulating the Distinction of Black Studies and the Study of Blacks: The Fundamental Role of Culture and the African-Centered Worldview." In *The African American Studies Reader*, ed. Nathaniel Norment Jr. 2nd ed. Durham, N.C.: Carolina Academic Press, 2007.

Baker, F. M. "Diagnosing Depression in African Americans." *Community Mental Health Journal* 37, no. 1 (2001): 31–38.

Bell, Bernard. *The Afro American Novel and Its Tradition.* Amherst: University of Massachusetts Press, 1987.

Bennefield, Robin M. "Black Feminist Foremothers." *Black Issues in Higher Education* 16, no. 7 (1999): 28.

Biegel, David E., Jeffrey A. Johnsen, and Robert Shafran. "Overcoming Barriers Faced by African-American Families with a Family Member with Mental Illness." *Family Relations* 46, no. 2 (1997): 163–178.

Boyd, Melba J. "Review Essay: Canon Configuration for Ida B. Wells-Barnett." *Black Scholar* 24, no. 1 (1994): 8–12.

Bradley, Stefan. "'Gym Crow Must Go!' Black Student Activism at Columbia University, 1967–1968." *Journal of African American History* 88, no. 2 (2003): 163–181.

Brown, Diane R., and Feroz Ahmed. "Major Depression in a Community Sample of African Americans." *American Journal of Psychiatry* 152, no. 3 (1995): 373–378.

Bunzel, John. "Black Studies at San Francisco State." In *The African American Studies Reader*, ed. Nathaniel Norment Jr. 2nd ed. Durham, N.C.: Carolina Academic Press, 2007.

Cade, Toni. *The Black Woman*. New York: Signet 1970.

Campbell, Bebe M. *Brothers and Sisters*. New York: G. P. Putnam's Sons, 1994.

———. *I Get So Hungry*. New York: G. P. Putnam's Sons, 2008.

———. Interview by Ashok Gangadean (*Global Lens*), February, 5, 2006. http://www.consciousnessprecedesmind.org/global-lens-channel/bebe-moore-campbell.html.

———. Interview by Bev Smith on *Our Voices*, (Black Entertainment Television), "Overcoming Life's Obstacles", n.d. (circa 1995). http://www.youtube.com/watch?v=yvxFsqvYje8.

———. Interview by *Time*, August 6, 2005. http://content.time.com/time/nation/article/0,8599,1090784,00.html.

———. *72 Hour Hold*. New York: Alfred A. Knopf, 2005.

———. *Singing in the Comeback Choir*. Vol. 381. New York: G. P. Putnam's Sons, 1998.

———. *Sometimes My Mommy Gets Angry*. New York: Puffin Books, 2003.

———. *Stompin' at the Savoy*. New York: Philomel Books, 2006.

———. *Successful Women, Angry Women*. New York: Jove Books, 1986.

———. *Sweet Summer: Growing Up with and without My Dad*. New York: G. P. Putnam's Sons, 1989.

———. *What You Owe Me*. New York: G. P. Putnam's Sons, 2001.

———. *Your Blues Ain't Like Mine*. New York: G. P. Putnam's Sons, 1992.

Campbell, Jane. "An Interview with Bebe Moore Campbell." *Callaloo: A Journal of African-American and African Arts and Letters* 22, no. 4 (Fall 1999): 954–972.

Campbell, Maia. Interview by Iyanla Vanzant on *Fix My Life* (Oprah Winfrey Network), November 17, 2012.

Christian, Barbara. *African American Women Novelists*. Westport, Conn.: Greenwood Press, 1980.

———, ed. *Black Feminist Criticism: Perspectives on Women Writers*. New York: Pergamon Press, 1985.

Clayborne, Carson. *In Struggle: SNCC and the Black Awakening of the 1960s*. Cambridge, Mass.: Harvard University Press, 1995.

Collins, Patricia Hill. *Black Feminist Thought: Knowledge, Consciousness, and the Politics of Empowerment*. New York: Routledge, 1991.

———. *Black Sexual Politics: African Americans, Gender, and the New Racism*. New York: Routledge, 2005.

Compton, Michael T., et al. "A Descriptive Study of Pathways to Care among Hospitalized Urban African American First-Episode Schizophrenia-Spectrum Patients." *Social Psychiatry & Psychiatric Epidemiology* 41, no. 7 (2006): 566–573.

Davis, Angela. "The Myth of the Black Rapist." In *Race, Women, and Class*. New York: Random House, 1981.

Diala, C., et al. "Racial Differences in Attitudes toward Professional Mental Health Care and in the Use of Services." *American Journal of Orthopyschiatry* 70, no. 4 (2000): 455–464.

Dragoin, Regina Maria. "Breaking the Ice: Representations of White Women in Civil Rights Movement Novels." PhD diss., Auburn University, 1999

Dubey, Madhu. *Black Women Novelists and the Nationalist Aesthetic*. Bloomington: Indiana University Press, 1994.

Duster, Alfreda M., and Ida B. Wells. *Crusade for Justice: The Autobiography of Ida B. Wells*. Chicago: University of Chicago Press, 1970.

Exum, William H. *Paradoxes of Protest: Black Student Activism in a White University*. Philadelphia: Temple University Press, 1985.

Fleming, Cynthia G. "Black Women Activists and the Student Nonviolent Coordinating Committee: The Case of Ruby Doris Smith Robinson." *Journal of Women's History* 4, no. 3 (1993): 31–54.

Funk, Michelle, et al. "Advocacy for Mental Health: Roles for Consumer and Family Organizations and Governments." *Health Promotion International* 21, no. 1 (2006): 70–75.

Gaines, Patricia. "A Writer for Our Time: Bebe Moore Campbell, 1950–2006." *Black Issues Book Review* 9, no. 1 (January/February 2007): 19.

Garretson, Deborah J. "Psychological Misdiagnosis of African Americans." *Journal of Multicultural Counseling & Development* 21, no. 2 (1993): 119–127.

Gayle, Addison. *The Black Aesthetic*. New York: Doubleday, 1971.

Giddings, Paula. *When and When I Enter: The Impact of Black Women on Race and Sex in America*. New York: Perennial, 1984.

Gillispie, Ricardo, Catherine Gillispie, and Edith Williams. "Hospitalized African American Mental Health Consumers: Some Antecedents to Service Satisfaction and Intent to Comply with Aftercare." *American Journal of Orthopsychiatry* 75, no. 2 (2005): 254–261.

Golafshani, Nahid. "Understanding Reliability and Validity in Qualitative Research." *Qualitative Report* 8, no. 4 (2003): 597–607.

Goldsmith, B., R. S. Morrison, L. C. Vanderwerker, and H. G. Prigerson. "Elevated Rates of Prolonged Grief Disorder in African Americans." *Death Studies* 32, no. 4 (2008): 352–365.

Hall, Stephanie Gail. "Coming Home: Homecomings and Return Migration in African-American Folklore and Literature since 1970." PhD diss., Louisiana State University and Agricultural & Mechanical College, 2000.

Hull, Gloria T., Patricia B. Scott, and Barbara Smith, eds. *All the Women Are White, All the Blacks Are Men, But Some of Us Are Brave: Black Women's Studies*. New York: Feminist Press, 1982.

James, Joy. "Resting in Gardens, Battling in Deserts: Black Women's Activism." *Black Scholar* 29, no. 4 (1999): 2–7.

Johnson-Fisher, Angela. *Afristocracy: Free Women of Color and the Politics of Race, Class, and Culture*. VDM Verlag, 2008.

Jones, Trevelyn E., et al. Review of *Black Women Activists* by Karin S. Codden. *School Library Journal* 50, no. 11 (2004): 162.

Joseph, Peniel E. "Dashikis and Democracy: Black Studies, Student Activism, and the Black Power Movement." *Journal of African American History* 88, no. 2 (2003): 182–203.

Karenga, Maulana. *Introduction to Black Studies*. Los Angeles: University of Sankore Press, 2002.

Knupfer, Anne Meis. "Private Politics and Public Voices: Black Women's Activism from World War I to the New Deal." *Journal of Southern History* 94, no. 3 (2007): 969.

Long, Richard A. "Black Studies Fall into Place." *Nation* 219, no. 1 (1974): 19–20.

Maddox, Alton H., Jr. "Black Women Have Given Us a Paradigm for Struggle." *New York Amsterdam News* 94, no. 12 (2003): 12.

Maxwell, Joseph. *Qualitative Research Design*. Thousand Oaks, Calif.: SAGE, 1996.

McCormick, Richard. *Black Students in Protest: A Study of the Origins of the Black Student Movement*. Newark, N.J.: University of Rutgers Press, 1990.

McCracken, Grant. 1988. *The Long Interview*. Thousand Oaks, Calif.: SAGE.

Meeks, Kenneth. "With Bebe Moore Campbell." *Black Enterprise*, April 2006. http://www.blackenterprise.com/2006/04/01/with-bebe-moore-campbell/.

"Mental Health Advocacy Group Critical of Lack of NIMH Research." *Brown University Psychopharmacology Update* 11, no. 2 (2000): 2.

Modleski, Tania. *Loving with a Vengeance: Mass-Produced Fantasies for Women*. New York: Routledge, 2008.

Muhammed, Khalil Gibran. *The Condemnation of Blackness: Race, Crime and the Making of Modern Urban America*. Cambridge, Mass.: Harvard University Press, 2003.

Neville, Helen A., and Jennifer F. Hamer. "Revolutionary Black Women's Activism: Experience and Transformation." *Black Scholar* 36, no. 1 (2006): 2–11.

Norment, Nathaniel, Jr., ed. *The African American Studies Reader*. 2nd ed. Durham, N.C.: Carolina Academic Press, 2007.

Perkins, Margo V. *Autobiography as Activism: Three Black Women of the Sixties*. Jackson: University Press of Mississippi, 2000.

Phillips, Layli. *The Womanist Reader: The First Quarter Century of Womanist Thought*. New York: Routledge, 2006.

Radway, Janice A. *Reading the Romance: Women, Patriarchy, and Popular Literature*. Chapel Hill: University of North Carolina Press, 1991.

Ransby, Barbara. "Black Feminism at Twenty-One: Reflections on the Evolution of a National Community." *Signs: Journal of Women in Culture & Society* 25, no. 4 (2000): 1215–1221.

Razza, Constance M. "Working Out: Middle-Class Black Women's 1990's Literature of Fitness, Health, and Community." PhD diss., University of California, Los Angeles, 2002.

Robnett, Belinda. *How Long, How Long: African American Women in the Struggle for Civil Rights*. New York: Oxford University Press, 1997.

Rogers, Elice E. "Afritics from Margin to Center: Theorizing the Politics of African American Women as Political Leaders." *Journal of Black Studies* 35, no. 6 (2005): 701–714.

Rojas, Fabio. *From Black Power to Black Studies: How a Radical Social Movement Became an Academic Discipline*. Baltimore: Johns Hopkins University Press, 2007.

Rooks, Noliwe. *White Money/Black Power: The Surprising History of African American Studies and the Crisis of Race in Higher Education*. Boston: Beacon Press, 2006.

Sanchez, Sonia. "The Impact of Bebe Moore Campbell on the African American and American Literary Genre." Presented at the Legacy Memorial Tribute Dinner, Sheraton Hotel Center City, Philadelphia, April 11, 2008.

Simien, Evelyn, and Rosalee A. Clawson "The Intersection of Race and Gender: An Examination of Black Feminist Consciousness, Race Consciousness, and Policy Attitudes." *Social Science Quarterly* 85, no. 3 (2004): 793–810.

Snow, David A., Louis A. Zurcger Jr., and Sheldon Eckland-Olsen. "Frame Alignment Processes, Micromobilization, and Movement Participation." *American Sociological Review* 1, no. 4 (1986): 464–481.

Soden-Harcum, Cindy Money. "The Dream Denied: The Effects of Migration on the African American Literary Character." Master's thesis, Morgan State University, 2002.

Sommer, Barbara, and Mary K. Quinlan. *The Oral History Manual*. Walnut Creek, Calif.: Altamira Press, 2002.

Springer, Kimberly. *Living for the Revolution: Black Feminist Organizations, 1968–1980*. Durham, N.C.: Duke University Press, 2006.

———. *Still Lifting Still Climbing*. New York: New York University Press, 1999.

Tewkesbury, Paul, III. "Writing the Beloved Community: Integrated Narratives in Six Contemporary American Novels about the Civil Rights Movement." PhD diss., Louisiana State University and Agricultural & Mechanical College, 2001.

Van Deburg, William L. *New Day in Babylon: The Black Power Movement and American Culture, 1965–1975*. Chicago: University of Chicago Press, 1992.

Walters, Ronald W. *White Nationalism/Black Interests: Conservative Public Policy and the Black Community*. Detroit: Wayne State University Press, 2003.

Welsh-Asante, Kariamu. *The African Aesthetic: Keeper of the Traditions*. Westport, Conn.: Greenwood Press, 1993.

Williams, Vernetta K. "Honor: A Double-Edged Sword. An Examination of the South's 'Culture of Honor': Wounding of Two Races." PhD diss., University of South Florida, 2007.

Williams-Forson, Psyche Aletheia. "Building Houses Out of Chicken Legs: African American Women, Material Culture, and the Powers of Self-Definition." PhD diss., University of Maryland, College Park, 2002.

Williamson, Joy A. *Black Power on Campus: The University of Illinois 1965–1975*. Urbana: University of Illinois Press, 2003.

Yee, Shirley J. "Gender Ideology and Black Women as Community-Builders in Ontario, 1850–70." *Canadian Historical Review* 75, no. 1 (1994): 53–73.

Zinn, Howard. *SNCC: The New Abolitionists*. Cambridge, Mass.: South End Press, 2002.

# Index

198